also from

aplomb publishing
San Francisco

Who Nuked the Duke?

What Ever Happened to Mommie Dearest?

Reel Horror - True Horrors Behind Hollywood's Scary Movies

Alfred Hitchcock: The Icon Years

Curse of the Silver Screen - Tragedy & Disaster Behind the Movies

Master of Disaster - Irwin Allen: The Disaster Years

Disaster on Film - Behind the Scenes of Hollywood's Classic Disaster Films

www.aplombpublishing.com

MOVIE STAR

&

THE MOBSTER

•

Lana Turner, Johnny Stompanato &
Homicide in the Pink Bedroom

By John William Law

aplomb publishing
San Francisco

Movie Star & The Mobster

Published by Aplomb Publishing, San Francisco, California.
Copyright 2016.

ISBN: 978-0-9892475-2-8

1st edition

Manufactured in the United States of America.

Dedicated to Lana Turner and her legion of fans.

"My life has been a series of emergencies."

- Lana Turner

TABLE of CONTENTS

Appendix

Movie Star & The Mobster

Acknowledgements

The facts detailed within the pages of this book come from several key sources. Lana Turner's autobiography, first published in 1982, and Cheryl Crane's account, published in her 1988 book, represent first-hand accounts of April 1958 events surrounding this story. This book may very well not have been possible without them. To capture the missing details of the case, police and autopsy and medical reports from 1958 were also used.

For the chronology of events that transpired over the days surrounding this tragedy, court and inquest transcripts were invaluable in capturing the various perspectives of the parties involved. All quotes are take verbatim from official transcripts where possible. Some audio and video interviews were also used to back up or reaffirm facts. News reports and other published accounts, most of which are included in the back of this book, provided detail and perspectives surrounding the case.

Special thanks to David Young for helping proof the manuscript and Dennis Constan for his keen eye to detail in editing the final draft. Additional thanks to *The Associated Press*, *The Los Angeles Times* and *Chicago Tribune* for some crime scene and courtroom photographs.

PREFACE

"I've always loved a challenge."
- Lana Turner

The dream factory of Hollywood made her a star, but what they got was much more than a pretty face. From a fabled and fabricated past, she would become an icon; but it was the story behind the screen that made her a legend.

OPENING REMARKS

I had reservations about tackling this project. It wasn't necessarily that I thought I was incapable of doing the topic justice; although I do count myself among the many writers with insecurities - never believing they've done as good a job as they hoped they'd do. However, having read and researched the topic enough, I felt I could tell a story not yet fully told – a story I certainly still believe was worth telling.

My reservations stemmed from bringing to light a topic that I suspect a lot of people might rather leave in its resting place. The idea of dredging up an ugly past, or somewhat disparaging memories of people who are no longer around to defend themselves might prove difficult and undesirable. With Cheryl Crane as the only living witness to the events that fateful April evening in Beverly Hills. What could be gained by returning to the scene of the crime after so much time?

Lana Turner had a lengthy and successful career as an actress. She graced the movie screen for nearly five decades and appeared on television and stage as well. She also took a crack at writing, authoring her autobiography on her life and career. To remember Lana Turner for one incident midway through her life, many of her staunchest supporters and fans have longed to have her achievements overshadow this rather tragic bookmark of sensationalism.

Some might even suggest that since both Cheryl Crane and Lana Turner offered their own accounts of the events that evening in April 1958 that the topic should be closed. In the end, as you will discover on the forthcoming pages, I decided to move ahead with the book, determined to report the full story.

Having been a newspaper reporter and journalist, I have a history of reporting events. In many cases, the stories reporters are tasked with reporting on are not always those we would choose to cover. I've had the fortune or misfortune of having to cover events like the plane crashes, murders, deaths of famous and infamous people. Asking difficult questions at a time of a tragedy can feel tragic in itself. I remember interviewing family members of a victim of the Lockerbie Scotland crash of Pan Am flight 103 on the anniversary of the terrorist act and talking to witnesses of the plane crash that killed Senator John Heinz in 1991. I also remember interviewing a man about his experiences in a Nazi concentration camp during

World War II and how those events had changed his life and the lives of those he cared for.

On the opposite end of the spectrum, I've also been forced to sit through small town school board meetings or local government functions where it can be more exciting to watch paint dry. I've had to try and pull a story out of nothing or interview a subject so boring that I could barely bring myself to sit down and cobble together a story someone would want to read. So, I've been accustomed at having to write about topics that I didn't always want write.

Where Lana Turner is concerned, I've been a fan for many years. I've seen the majority of her nearly 60 films as well as television appearances. Some I've seen many, many times. I've read the books, the magazine articles, and viewed the documentaries that chronicle her life.

The period that began in the spring of 1957 - when she met a man named John Steele, and climax with his death roughly a year later - would mark the darkest period she would face as a woman and a mother. Martin Luther King once said,

> LANA TURNER'S LIFE – AND CAREER – CAN, IN MANY WAYS BE MEASURED BY HOW SHE CARRIED HERSELF THROUGH THIS DARK PERIOD.

"The true measure of a man is not how he behaves in moments of comfort and convenience, but how he stands at times of controversy and challenges." Lana Turner's life – and career – can, in many ways be measured by how she carried herself through this dark period.

In the end I ultimately asked myself two questions – questions I often ask myself before I tackle a book. First, is the story I want to tell something different than any other story out there? While the story hasn't changed in the nearly 60 years since the events of 1958, and the saga had been written about before, my goal was to approach the story from a different perspective. Lana Turner and her daughter Cheryl Crane both offered their own perspectives on "the paragraph," as they often referred to the events that night. And while their stories took us inside the tragedy in very personal ways, they were broader stories covering their lives and many experiences and events. Several other books looked at the story, but it was only one of a number of stories covering Hollywood scandals.

The second question I ask myself is, if this book were written by someone other than me, is it a story that I'd want to read. Without a doubt, I find the story a fascinating one, and it is very much the type of story I love to read about. With more than a half century having passed since that fateful night the story has become part of Hollywood history.

My goal was to look at the events that night and how it shaped the life and career of Lana Turner. The image of the glamorous movie star had already begun to change as she approached 40. The roles that she was being offered were moving away from those of the screen goddess that made her famous. As the mother of a teenage daughter, her role in *Peyton Place* would take on a whole new perspective after April 1958, and the part she would take on after that would often be much closer to her own life.

Whether it was dealing with troubled teens, dangerous lovers or murder, her best-known films from this period of her career earned their attention by reminding moviegoers of her past. Though, Turner would tackle each role for what it was and leveraged her talent and beauty to draw fans in and experience Lana the star.

For Lana Turner was a survivor and she mustered her

strength, gathered whatever courage she had, and used the intelligence and wisdom within her to find her way though the darkness. It is this Lana Turner and this story I hope you'll discover with me.

- John William Law

ONE

" I liked the boys and the boys liked me."

- Lana Turner

From a teenager sipping a soda to the "sweater girl" to screen siren, femme fatale, movie goddess and icon, Lana Turner epitomized the Hollywood dream - and the high price that came with it.

INTRODUCTION

"For three ghastly heartbeats our bodies fused," Cheryl Crane said of the night of April 4, 1958. That night, the lives of three people were forever altered. One would die; one would be scarred by a killing ... and the third, in many ways, would be reborn.

Johnny Stompanato could rarely be called a good man, but as a gangster he was never the villain as some attempted to portray him. He was tall, powerful, handsome and sexy to many he encountered. He also held a bit of mystery and danger. These were the traits that drew Lana Turner to him. He would die that night.

Stompanato was drawn to Lana Turner for many reasons as well. Simply enough, she was gorgeous, sexy, and a movie star. A blonde bombshell, she was the type of woman most men desired. She was also wealthy – a trait that Johnny Stompanato also found very attractive. She fell for his charms and strength. She liked the idea of a big strong man being in charge, and Johnny liked to take charge. He just didn't count on her daughter.

Cheryl would forever be marred by the tragic events that evening. She's later said that there was never a time in her life – after that night – when the mention of her name wouldn't be followed by the fact that she was the girl that killed Lana Turner's lover. She would be dragged through the mud of court proceedings, made a ward of the state and sent to boarding school where trouble with the law would continue to follow her. She found it difficult to put the events behind her, but ultimately would have to accept the tragedy of that night.

As a daughter, she would struggle – as many children of celebrities do – for the attention and love of what some have called a vain or self-absorbed movie star. While no one would doubt Lana loved her daughter, her ability to parent was clearly called into question. There were times when Cheryl may have been more a parent than Lana would be. On that night in April 1958, Cheryl's need to protect and to defend her mother was combined with her unwillingness to give up what little attention she had from Lana. She wasn't about to let Johnny Stompanato take that away.

Lana, some might say, was reborn that evening. Her career had been teetering on the edge of a precipice. As an aging sex symbol, closing in on 40, Lana was thought by many to be washed up. Though she found herself at the peak of success with an Oscar nomination that year, there was much question as to what would come next. How could she keep that momentum with no real movie prospects in her immediate future? Her personal life was a mess. She faced a difficult relationship with her ex-husband, a teenage daughter detracting from her glamorous sex symbol persona, and a lover who was demanding control of her every move and threatening to kill her

Lana Turner, the star, in a studio publicity shot.

if she ever tried to leave him. It was a tragedy waiting to happen, but it was often unclear as to who would end up the tragic figure in the drama.

Originally introduced to Lana Turner as John Steele, Johnny Stompanato was known in part for his good looks and sexual prowess with the ladies. Powerfully built and with a deep baritone voice, Stompanato spoke in short sentences, reportedly due to his poor grasp of proper grammar. He could be cold in many ways. He seldom laughed out loud and rarely smiled. Some said that he had a temper. Cheryl Crane remembered him as "always coiled, holding himself in" with "watchful hooded eyes that took in more than he wanted anyone to notice."

Stompanato also had a tough guy image and a reputation as a hood connected to organized crime and the Los Angeles underworld. He had a sketchy past, with some fudging of the facts to make him look a bit more heroic and polished than he really was. His business dealings, some say, were more of a smokescreen used to hide his hoodlum activities and his less-than-honest work for gangster Mickey Cohen. He also liked the idea of living the good life and walking alongside the rich and famous. He would look for any means to do so, even if it meant intimidation or petty theft from the women with whom he became involved.

In contrast, Lana Turner was a movie queen who ignited the silver screen with her sultry good looks, hourglass figure and warm, bubbly personality. The story Hollywood spun was that she was discovered at the soda counter in Schwab's Drugstore, destined for fame. In reality, it wasn't a drug store, but rather a coffee house. In 1936 while enrolled at Hollywood High School, she decided one day to skip class, and opted to sneak across the street to the Top Hat Cafe for a soda. It was here she was discovered.

"I had been going there less than a month when I decided to cut typing class and run across Highland for a soda. Not a strawberry soda or a chocolate malted, the way the story goes. It was only a Coke, because Coke cost a nickel, and that was all the money I had," Turner recalled.

After her "discovery" she quickly found her face and figure getting noticed by movie makers and fans, as well as the tabloids. Men either adored her or lusted after her – or both. By the age of 19 she was married to the first of seven husbands. In addition to the husbands, the starlet and movie goddess would attract countless suitors, beaus and lovers, including Tyrone Power, Fernando Lamas and John Steele (aka Johnny Stompanato).

Lana signed a long-term film contract with MGM at the age of sixteen, and appeared in her first movie *They Won't Forget* in 1937. Soon she was landing supporting roles in a host of MGM features, including *Love Finds Andy Hardy* in 1938, *The Adventures of Marco Polo* (1938), *These Glamour Girls* (1939), *Dancing Co-Ed* (1939), *Two Girls on Broadway* (1940), and *Ziegfeld Girl* (1941). With *Dr. Jekyll and Mr. Hyde* (1941), *Johnny Eager* (1941), and *Somewhere I'll Find You (*1942), she would begin to establish herself as a leading lady and a legitimate actress as well as star.

Her years of being known as "The Sweater Girl" for her figure would begin to be shed in 1948, when she starred opposite John Garfield as the femme fatale in *The Postman Always Rings Twice.* One of the quintessential film noir pictures, the movie would turn her into a screen icon, earn her greater roles and solidify her stardom. More success followed with films like *The Three Musketeers* (1948), *The Bad and the Beautiful* (1952) and *The Sea Chase* (1955), opposite John Wayne. She tried her hand at a period epic with *The Prodigal* in 1955, but the film and her performance were not well received.

"I finally got tired of making movies where all I did was walk across the screen and look pretty. I got a big chance to do some real acting in *The Postman Always Rings Twice*, and I'm not going to slip back if I can help it," she once said. "I tried to persuade the studio to give me something different. But every time I went into my argument about how bad a picture was they'd say, 'well, it's making a fortune.' That licked me."

In 1956 she would star in *Diane*, an historical film drama about the life of Diane de Poitiers, produced by MGM. Directed by David Miller, Turner starred opposite Roger Moore and Pedro Armendáriz, with the story taking place in 16th century France. As Diane de Poitiers, Turner spends most of the film manipulating the men in her life to obtain power and success.

Johnny Stompanato was one of the patrons who saw the film after its release that year. He was so taken with the star that he reportedly purchased the named Rowena, on which she rode sidesaddle in the film. He began to set his sights on meeting the star and would use the horse to ingratiate himself not only with Lana, but with her teenage daughter, Cheryl, as well.

Diane would become both a turning point professionally and personally for Lana. Besides leading to her tumultuous relationship with Stompanato, it also led to the end of her relationship with MGM. The studio decided not to renew her contract after the film was released in 1956, ending her nearly 20 years with the studio. MGM-Lowes lost money for the first time in its history that year, coming in $455,000 in the red, the studio subsequently made many cuts in areas where it didn't see enough return on its investment. It was a tough period for all the studios as TV began to cut into their profits, but it hit some studios like MGM harder as government regulations began to force them to divest themselves of their movie theater businesses. Lana's career was over the studio thought.

Lana Turner, however, was not one to give up easily. She quickly lined up work for herself with two competing studios. *The Lady Takes a Flyer,* for Universal, would be released in January 1958. *Peyton Place*, from Twentieth-Century Fox, would be filmed after, was released just prior in December 1957. The features would offer the promise of career survival for the Hollywood veteran, but they were also created under a time of great duress for the star. However, Lana was a survivor.

This period would represent a major turning point for the Hollywood leading lady. While it would present her with the greatest critical and financial success of her career, it would also mark one of the darkest and personally challenging times in her life.

Producer Robert Evans once said, "There are three sides to every story - yours ... mine ... and the truth." He could easily have been referring to the story surrounding Lana Turner's romance with – and the death of – Johnny Stompanato, inside her plush pink bed-room.

Two

"That walk down the street of a Southern town would completely change my life."

- Lana Turner on 'They Won't Forget'

He lay there motionless on the plush carpeted floor of the pretty pink bedroom. Quiet gasps in the final moments of his life were all he offered. Time seemed to tick by slowly, but the thoughts wouldn't seem to come to her. She stood there frozen, not quite sure what to do or what had actually just happened.

The EARLY YEARS

"In that instant of consciousness a wave of shock hit me," she recalled years later. "I stared at Cheryl as she dropped the knife and began to cry. Numbly, I turned to look at John as he lay motionless on the floor. Then, I took Cheryl by the shoulder and sent her to her room. John was making dreadful, soft, choking sounds. I went to him and leaned over, but I didn't see a wound. Not until I lifted his sweater. It was a small wound, only a little slice. Strangely there was very little blood."

The stab wound may have been small, but the damage was not. Penetrating the liver and cutting through the abdominal aorta, the largest artery in the abdominal cavity, the wound brought on a massive hemorrhage. Internal bleeding would have hidden the seriousness of the stabbing. As the victim lay on his back, the bleeding would have traveled with gravity toward the back. With no means of escape it would remain inside him. Though blood may have remained absent, the seriousness of his injuries was all too real. He would be dead in a matter of minutes.

As this dark figure in her life died before her, Lana Turner once again faced the violent death of an important man in her life.

Tragedy at an Early Age

At the intersection of Minnesota and Mariposa streets on the southern edge of San Francisco's waterfront, a body was discovered in the early morning hours of December 14, 1930. In what at first

The San Francisco intersection where Lana Turner's father was found dead in 1930.

appeared to be a couple of a few rumpled sacks of potatoes, John Turner's body was left lying at the side of the street. He had been beaten to death with a blunt object about the head and face. Missing one shoe and sock, police were stumped as to who had killed him and why. Nevertheless, they located his wife, Mildred, and delivered the tragic news. Then, they looked to piece together the events that led to his death by discovering who John Turner was.

John Turner and Mildred Turner met around 1919 in Oklahoma when she was just 15 and he was 24. Mildred Frances Cowan was born in Lamar, Arkansas and was raised by her father and a great-aunt, her father's mother's sister. John Turner hailed from Montgomery, Alabama where he served as an infantry platoon sergeant during World War I, earning several medals for valor. Recently out of the Army he worked as a miner, but headed west looking for more. According to Lana, it was in Picher, Oklahoma, in a roof garden restaurant, where he saw young Mildred, who was traveling with her father, a mining engineer, in town to conduct an inspection of the local mine. Turner asked the young girl to dance and quickly the two fell in love. When he asked her father if he could court her, her father said no. Not to be deterred, the young lovers ran off and eloped in 1920.

About a year later, a daughter, Julia Jean Mildred Frances Turner, was born on February 8, 1921 in Wallace, Idaho. There was a great deal of concern and worry as she entered the world. Her grandmother had died in childbirth due to Rh factor complications, and the condition may have been passed to her daughter Mildred. However, Lana, as she would later be known, came into the world easily and her mother and father welcomed her with open arms. Her parents nicknamed her Judy.

In her autobiography, Lana recalled her early childhood years with her parents fondly. Evenings, after dinner, were spent dancing and listening to records. She would say that her lifelong love of music and dance came from those early years. Even though her parents didn't have much, she never felt it was a struggle. Her father spent his days working in the mines to earn a living, but was also a bit of a gambler who happened to be "an excellent card player." His skills helped support the family through rough times.

Some reports suggest that John Turner was more than just a bit of a gambler. He was also a bootlegger and a small-time crook. His scuffles with the law had him changing his name, along with his wife's and daughter's as they made their way from town to town, always trying to keep one step ahead of the police, or anyone else who might be on their heels.

In 1927, when Judy Turner was six years old, John Turner piled his wife and daughter in their car - along with whatever belongings they could carry - and headed for San Francisco. She remembered sitting between her parents during the long car drive, as well as on his lap as he drove. She even recounted his letting her put her hands on the wheel and his falling asleep as she drove the car, until her mother looked over and grabbed the wheel.

Life in San Francisco, however, failed to deliver on the promise of success for the small family. They lived in a series of small, furnished rooms for a time and then in a small house in Stockton, California. To make ends meet, John Turner made moonshine in the basement of their home during prohibition. After police caught on, Turner was without an income and found it difficult to find work. To cover expenses, he began taking part in small card games in San Francisco. Lana didn't remember much of his gambling, but would recall later that it was during this time that her parents separated, and her mother found work in a San Francisco beauty parlor. Mother and daughter relocated to the city.

"When I asked my mother where he'd gone, she said that he was traveling, selling insurance."

She said her parents never divorced. When her mother later found better work in Sacramento, the pair moved there, however setbacks caused them to return to San Francisco where they shared a small apartment with two young women. Lana's room was really just a closet and eventually Mildred found a home in Stockton for Lana to live in. A couple took young Lana in allowing her to share a room with their young daughter. In addition to having a playmate about her age she had a backyard to play in. Her mother visited every other week, but she seldom saw her father.

On one of the last visits she had with her father she asked him to get her a bicycle. Not long after her father was reportedly killed after a card game in San Francisco.

John Turner was last seen at a traveling crap game in the building of *The San Francisco Chronicle* in downtown San Francisco on the night of December 14, 1930. After winning at the end of the evening he bragged about using his winnings to buy a bike for his daughter. The bike would never be purchased though, because later that evening he would be robbed and murdered. His body was found by police miles away from where he had last been seen. Police later suspected that his winnings had been stashed in the sock and shoe of his left foot. When they found him his head had been crushed by a blackjack and he was missing his left sock and shoe. His death would remain unsolved.

As young as she was at the time, Julia didn't really grasp the loss of a father might have on her. For the remainder of her life, she would be drawn to strong men who would provide her with the emotional security a father figure might. The protection, strength, and control these men would have over her would be a guiding force in her life.

To make ends meet, her mother would struggle to find work and to provide a stable, safe home for her daughter. Whether in San

Francisco, Stockton, or Sacramento, the Turner women lived pay-check to paycheck and struggled to get by.

One thing young Julia found as a distraction from her difficult childhood was her love of the movies. She would save a nickel of her lunch money every day to save enough to purchase a 25-cent

In the early days, Lana on the rise as a star at MGM.

ticket to the Saturday matinee. She would find herself drawn to the elaborate costumes of leading ladies like Kay Francis and Norma Shearer and even once said that if she hadn't gone into movies, she probably would have tried her hand at being a fashion designer.

In search of better opportunities, Julia's mother decided southern California might be worth a shot and moved herself and her daughter to Los Angeles. Shortly after their arrival, fifteen-year-old Julia cut typing class and ran across the street, sneaking out of school to go for a Coke.

Despite the legend, she didn't head to Schwab's Drugstore, but The Top Hat Café, a shop across the street from Hollywood High. She didn't go for a malt because she only had a nickel, and that was the price of a Coca Cola.

When W.R. Wilkerson, publisher of *The Hollywood Reporter*, happened into the cafe and caught sight of young Julia, he introduced himself, gave her his card and asked her to call newly operating talent agent and actor/comedian, Zeppo Marx. After consulting with her mother, she made the call. Soon after Marx's new agency signed her on as a client. She reportedly had her first walk on part as an extra in *A Star is Born* in 1937, starring Janet Gaynor and Frederick March. However, it was after Marx introduced her to film director Mervyn LeRoy, who was casting for the film, *They Won't Forget,* also in 1937, that her life changed.

LeRoy said she was "too scared to look like a star or even a potential star" when first I met her. "I was casting for *They Won't Forget*. I had interviewed over a hundred girls, and none seemed suited for the role I had in mind. Then Solly Biano, a Warner's talent scout, reported that a friend of ours, Billy Wilkerson, editor and publisher of the film trade paper *The Hollywood Reporter* had tipped him about a girl he had seen having a soda across the street from his publishing firm."

When he met her, LeRoy said "she was as scared as a rabbit;

but I knew she'd make a good actress. So I signed her to a personal contract and put her into a sweater - the former was good business; the latter was what the customers wanted to see. The rest is all history."

As for her name, it was quickly decided it required a change. However, there are a few different versions of who decided on the change. Leroy claimed that he felt Judy, her nickname, was too plain, and Julia Jean wasn't right either. LeRoy suggested Leonore, but it was Julia/Judy who said, "What about ... Lana?" She spelled it for LeRoy and waited while he said it several times finally nodding in agreement. "That's it," Leroy replied. "You're Lana Turner."

THREE

"Well, I'm going up and up and up--and nobody's going to pull me down!"

- Lana Turner as Lora Meredith
in 'Imitation of Life'

As a movie goddess, Lana Turner reigned as one of MGM's brightest and most popular of stars. Her success, some say, was in part due to her story as a small-town girl who makes it big. But with her highs, came dark and difficult lows. Her pop cultural icon status was as much for what she left on screen as for tragic and stormy moments off screen.

CAREER ON THE RISE

Lana related to the role of schoolgirl Mary Clay in *They Won't Forget*, and it proved to be a valuable introduction to the industry and with moviegoers as well. With a part small but central to the story, she found it easy to play. She had few lines, but lit up the screen and showed off both her beauty and her figure.

The Hollywood Reporter noticed her immediately, writing, "Short on playing time is the role of the murdered school girl. But as played by Lana Turner, it is worthy of more than passing note. This young lady has vivid beauty, personality and charm."

With a small part and little opportunity for acting in the film, she found herself praised for her proportions and was tagged "The Sweater Girl," due to the tight wool sweater she had worn in the film.

"I made my first movie without ever considering that my walk-on would be anything more than a one-time job," Lana recalled thinking after completing her first picture. "If I could have foreseen

A star spokesperson appearing in a 1950s magazine ad.

everything that was going to happen to me; all the headlines my life would make; all the people who would pass through my days, I wouldn't have believed a syllable of it!"

Her next film, *The Great Garrick,* was another LeRoy effort and after finishing it, she was loaned to MGM for *The Adventures of Marco Polo.* During the filming, Samuel Goldwyn insisted Lana's eyebrows be shaved off and replaced with straight, fake black ones. They never grew back, and from then on she had to either paste on or draw in eyebrows.

LeRoy left Warner Bros for MGM and took Lana with him, doubling her salary from $50 to $100 a week. Lana used the money to buy a house in Brentwood for her and her mother. As her fame grew, so did her salary, and by the time she was 20, she was earning $1,500 a week at MGM and was one of their brightest stars. Soon she was being recognized on the street, but she found a way to escape fans. She recalled years later, if someone recognized her while she was out, she would often reply, "Oh, no, no. I've been told I look like her."

At MGM, Lana would make most of her memorable films, beginning in 1938 with *Love Finds Andy Hardy.* It would be followed by a string of films where she often played supporting roles, until *These Glamour Girls* in 1939. After this film she would be the leading lady of most of her pictures, from *Ziegfeld Girl* in 1941, to *Honky Tonk*, also in 1941, *Johnny Eager* in 1942, *Slightly Dangerous* in 1943, and *Marriage is a Private Affair* in 1944. She co-starred alongside Laraine Day and Susan Peters in 1945's *Keep Your Powder Dry* and with Ginger Rogers in 1945's *Weekend at the Waldorf.*

During World War II, Lana participated in railroad tours selling war bonds. She even promised "a sweet kiss" to any man who purchased a bond worth $50,000 or more. She reportedly kept the promise on a number of occasions, once saying, "I'm told I increased the defense budget by several million dollars."

She renegotiated her MGM contract in 1945 pushing her salary to $4,000 a week and took a starring role in *The Postman Always Rings Twice*. The film noir feature was dark and gritty and gave her a dramatic part she could sink her teeth into and get noticed for her acting and not just her figure. "Finally, the part I had been hoping for did

The Hollywood goddess in a studio glamour shot.

come my way," she recalled.

In 1948, she made *The Three Musketeers*, and it would mark her first Technicolor picture. Playing opposite Vincent Price, she enjoyed working with him. "I studied him, and it challenged me, and I began to try things I never knew I could do," she said. "I found my own little touches-a certain sly look, the flap of a glove, a tilt of the head."

Lana's next major film to test her acting abilities had her starring opposite Kirk Douglas in *The Bad and The Beautiful*. The film went on to win five Academy Awards, including best screenplay and best costumes.

Latin Lovers in 1953 cast her opposite Ricardo Montalban for the first time, and in *Betrayed* in 1954, she shared the big screen for the last of four times with Clark Gable.

As MGM began to struggle in the mid-1950s it loaned Turner out to other studios for pictures. In 1955, she returned to Warner Bros., the studio that first put her on the big screen. She starred opposite John Wayne in *The Sea Chase*. Later that year she would be loaned to Twentieth-Century Fox for *The Rains of Ranchipur*. She would return to MGM for *Diane* in 1956, but the film would mark the end of her career with the studio. Lana was released from her contract after the film. She would actually film *The Rains of Ranchipur* after making *Diane*, and because she was on loan from MGM it was the official final film of her contract, but *Diane* would be the last film she'd make for the studio.

During these years, Lana's personal life often got in the way of her career. Costars claimed that Lana could be unprofessional or unfocused on the set, and this criticism, tied with the lackluster performance of her films. It would be part of the reason that Lana was considered a fading star by the mid-1950s. Some called her a deeply troubled star whose recent years had been scarred by "soured love affairs, migraine headaches, divorces, miscarriages, a suicide attempt, and IRS problems."

If that weren't bad enough, her drinking had become a problem. During 1955's *The Sea Chase*, starring opposite John Wayne, Lana began missing morning calls to the set. When she did show up, she was nursing a hangover. After the third late arrival she was fired by director John Farrow, but she managed to convince John Wayne that she deserved a second chance and he intervened and got her back on the set. She tried to control her behavior, but the movie still suffered at the box office.

While Lana was churning out films, she was also churning out husbands. There would be a total of seven husbands. At one time or another, Lana was linked to nearly every eligible bachelor or

Cheryl, Lana and Lana's Mother, Mildred, with Lana appearing to have it all.

up and coming actor in Hollywood. Many, like Tyrone Power, were legitimate romances, but others were more publicity – either for Lana or for the male suitor – than they were real. Lana liked men, and men liked her.

"My goal was to have one husband and seven children, but it turned out to be the other way around," Lana once remarked years later, reflecting on her string of failed marriages and desire for stable family life. It was out of this desire that she found herself often in the company of men. Rarely "single," Lana was well known for dating a string of men. Her beauty, fame and popularity made it easy to find available partners – if not long lasting ones.

Prior to her marriage to Stephen Crane and the birth of their daughter, Lana's first marriage to band leader and composer Artie Shaw ended within seven months in 1940. Though Shaw was more than a decade older than Lana the couple reportedly eloped on their first date in what would become a highly publicized romance. It was the third of eight marriages for Shaw and ended with tales of abuse. Lana referred to her first marriage as her "college education." She was only 19 at the time.

Her marriage to Crane would have been equally short-lived had it not been for the birth of their daughter. "He mentioned nonchalantly that he was in the tobacco business, in a way that suggested that any kind of business bored him. Certainly it seemed that he had no money worries. We chatted for hours, and by the time he took me home, I was ready to fall in love. With my weakness for a certain kind of good looks, coupled with witty charm, I took him at face value. In no time, we were a pair. Only three weeks later, he asked me to marry him," Lana recalled.

The marriage began with high hopes in July 1942; but by the end of the year it was revealed that Crane's divorce from his first wife had never been finalized, Lana had the marriage annulled in early 1943. Lana learned she was pregnant in December 1942. So once Crane was legally free of his first marriage, he and Lana wed for a second time in March 1943 in Tijuana, Mexico. Their daughter, Cheryl Christine Crane, was born in July 1943. However, wedded bliss was not to be and Lana filed for divorce in April 1944. The divorce became final that August.

In 1948, Lana met Henry J. "Bob" Topping Jr., grandson of tin plate magnate Daniel G. Reid and brother of New York Yankees owner Dan Topping. Topping asked Turner to marry him by dropping a diamond ring into her martini during dinner at the 21 Club. She said yes and the wedding came three days after Topping was divorced from his third wife. Reportedly worth millions when they married, Topping would incur heavy financial losses from poor investments and rumors of excessive gambling. They divorced in 1952.

Within a year, Lana was on to husband number four. Actor Lex Barker was the lucky man. Best known for playing Tarzan, the Ape Man in five films, it was Barker's third marriage and came on the heels of his divorce from actress Arlene Dahl. Lana wed Barker in the fall of 1952, and the marriage lasted until July 1957.

Without the support of a studio or a solid marriage, Lana needed to fend for herself and to find work elsewhere. While her career would go on to new and better heights, it would also kick off one of the darkest periods of her life when a dark figure offering charm, passion and mystery swept Lana off her feet.

FOUR

"I'm so gullible. I'm so damn gullible.
And I am so sick of me being gullible."
                                    - Lana Turner

Los Angeles of the 1950s was home to a high-profile mob presence. LA Gang boss, Mickey Cohen, may have had a target on his back for bombs or guns; but he also had the ear of the media and the reputation of a local celebrity, not unlike the stars with whom he crossed paths.

A DEADLY ENCOUNTER

While Lana Turner would suggest that her nefarious entanglement with Johnny Stompanato was her first and only encounter with members of organized crime, it wasn't entirely true. Hollywood, practically since its inception, was closely acquainted with the darker side of Los Angeles. And Lana was, at times, closer than she might have ever even realized.

Bugsy Siegel was a well-connected player in Hollywood

who carried a lot of muscle. As a key figure in LA's organized crime family, Siegel would intersect with Lana Turner on various fronts. He was born in New York in 1906 as Benjamin Siegel, but quickly came to be known as Bugsy. After dropping out of school, he joined a gang on Manhattan's Lower East Side and elevated quickly from small thefts to a practice of "protection and extortion." His racket consisted of forcing pushcart merchants to pay him and his fellow gangsters, or they would set fire to their property and goods.

By his teens, his criminal record included armed robbery, rape and murder. He soon made the leap to New York's bevy of mobsters and would climb the ranks until he learned his enemies were planning to kill him. To stay alive, he relocated to California in 1930 where the East Coast mob gave him the chance to set up syndicate gambling rackets with Los Angeles crime family boss, Jack Dragna. In addition to gambling and racketeering, they also dabbled in prostitution.

Through connections with local politicians, attorneys, accountants and lobbyists, he found himself often in the company of Hollywood's elite - studio heads Louis B. Mayer and Jack Warner and celebrities that included Clark Gable, Gary Cooper and Cary Grant, Jean Harlow and more. Beautiful young starlets, including Lana Turner, were often found at studio events mingling with local mobsters in attendance.

Siegel's plans focused on extorting movie studios by taking over local unions like The Screen Extras Guild and the Los Angeles Teamsters. He'd drive the unions to stage strikes and get the studios to pay to get the unions back to work.

Things began to unravel for Siegel in late 1939 when he was implicated in the murder of Harry Greenberg after Greenberg threatened to become a police informant. Siegel hired defense attorney Jerry Giesler, a man Lana would later turn to as well. After the deaths of several witnesses, Siegel was acquitted due to lack of evidence. However, his name, face and reputation were now too well known and he was becoming a liability in the Los Angeles crime world. In 1944, he was arrested for bookmaking, but was acquitted.

After his arrest, Siegel decided he wanted to become legitimate and looked at Las Vegas as a chance to start over. He used the Flamingo Hotel as a launching pad, but found escape from a life of organized crime a difficult one. Soon, criminal activity began to creep in. Siegel spent his time moving between Las Vegas and Los Angeles, but his lavish spending to build his new gambling enterprise irked his crime counterparts and he needed more and more money to keep going.

The Flamingo held a splashy opening that included a collection of Hollywood stars like George Raft, Rose Marie, and Jimmy Durante who performed that night as well as guests, including Clark Gable, Cesar Romero, Judy Garland, Joan Crawford. Lana Turner was also in attendance for the opening. However the hotel was still unfinished.

On June 20, 1947, Siegel was shot multiple times in the Beverly Hills home of his girlfriend, Virginia Hill. The home on Linden Drive was only about a minute drive from the North Bedford Drive home Lana would move into years later. No one was ever charged with the murder, and the crime remains unsolved, though some suggest that his lavish spending on the Flamingo and possible skimming of mob money led to a contract being put on his life.

For Lana, Siegel's death might have gone unnoticed, but the man who took his place was a man named Mickey Cohen. Cohen had been Siegel's second in command back in 1939. It was Cohen who helped orchestrate the Flamingo Hotel deal and build a lucrative sports booking operation in Las Vegas. Cohen climbed the ranks after Siegel's demise, but his violent behavior and outbursts earned him a host of enemies and numerous attempts on is life. Cohen hired a tall, dark and handsome man named Johnny Stompanato to act as his bodyguard. In addition to looking out for Cohen, Stompanato dabbled in sexual extortions of the Hollywood elite. Once he set his sights on Lana Turner, she would find herself literally in bed with the West Coast mob.

Stompanato once claimed his association with Mickey Cohen went as far back as his Marine Corps service during World War II, but other reports suggest it began around 1947 when he arrived in Hollywood.

By 1955, Mickey Cohen was known by many insiders as "The King of Hollywood Underworld," and Stompanato was looking at The Myrtlewood Gift Shop in the Westwood area of Los Angeles as a cover for his underworld activities. The store sold cheap pottery and other art, but really was nothing more than a place for Stompanato to call his "place of work." His two-year marriage to Helen Stanley, a 26-year-old actress was in the process of ending and he would soon be looking for her replacement.

First working under the name Dolores Diane, Stanley began work at the age of 14 in 1942's *Girls' Town,* and worked regularly in small or uncredited roles throughout the 1940s in mostly B-pictures. Appearing in films for Universal, MGM and Twentieth-Century Fox, her best films came between 1949 and 1952 in small parts or walk-ons in features like *All the Kings Men, The Asphalt Jungle* and *The Snows of Kilimanjaro*. Her relationship

Johnny Stompanato

with Stompanato began in 1952. He saw her as an opportunity to marry a pretty young starlet who might help pay his way and get him closer to the inner Hollywood circle. He proposed in December and they married in early 1953. Stanley's career, though, never took off and by 1955, Stanley was finding most of her work in television in small parts on shows like *Big Town, Walt Disney's Wonderful World of Color, Lux Video Theatre* and *I Led 3 Lives*.

By early 1955, Stanley had filed for divorce from Stompanato and Lana was in the middle of a four-year marriage to *Tarzan's* Lex Barker. Though her marriage was still going strong, her career was a bit more uncertain. As the Hollywood studio system began to collapse with anti-trust laws forcing the major players to sell off their theater chains, their financials began to suffer and their control over stars began to wane. Some stars left studios willingly looking for more control over their careers and the films they made, while others were cast aside because they were too costly to keep. Contract players like Lana were removed from the studio books and hired only on a film-by-film basis. For Lana, the uncertainty of a regular paycheck left her concerned about her livelihood. With her mother and daughter to care for and a lavish lifestyle to which she was accustomed, she had to take on more responsibility for earning a living.

When MGM cut Lana loose after the filming of *Diane* in 1955 she fortunately had a couple more films left to make under her contract. One of those would be on loan to Twentieth-Century Fox. While Fox would release *The Rains of Ranchipur* during Christmas of 1955, *Diane* wouldn't hit screens until January 1956. Aside from the release date, Lana wouldn't work on a film for more than a year. Without a studio behind her, she had to regroup and find some strong allies who could help her define what was left of her career.

Even with her film career in question, she was still one of Hollywood's biggest stars and earned attention wherever she appeared. Newspapers and magazines continued to report on her every move - so much so that on national television on November 27, 1955 she received an award from Dell Publishing Company as "The star who appeared on the most fan magazine covers."

Though she'd appear as herself in a 1956 episode of the TV series *Climax!*, she'd spend most of the time looking for a suitable film project with the help of her agent, Paul Kohner. Universal would give Lana that project with *The Lady Takes a Flyer* in early 1957. Production would begin that spring. It's worth noting that the film wouldn't be released until January 1958, following on the heels of the Christmas 1957 release of the successful *Peyton Place*, a film Lana would tackle after completing *The Lady Takes a Flyer*.

The Lady Takes a Flyer, according to Universal publicity, was in part based on true events and detailed the lives of Mary and Jack Ford, who were known in flying circles as "the flying Fords." It tells the story of a daredevil pilot, Mike Dandridge, who enters a business partnership with his flight-school buddy. He meets Maggie Colby, played by Lana, who's also a pilot. Mike hires Maggie to fly cargo to Japan and soon the two become romantically involved. After marrying, Maggie becomes pregnant, and Mike expects her to give up her career and focus on motherhood. As she begins to settle down he goes off and hires another female pilot to take her place. At home with their daughter, Maggie begins to suspect Mike might be having an affair with his new pilot while away on business trips. Maggie decides to resume her flying career and leaves Mike caring for their daughter as she heads off on a flight to England, but Mike decides to beat her to London and takes a risk by bringing the baby along on his flight to Europe.

Drama ensues when Mike arrives first and Maggie's plane encounters difficulty landing in thick London fog after the runway is closed. Mike instructs her to parachute from her crippled plane before it crashes. Mike and Maggie are brought closer by the experience.

Produced by Universal-International, it was an important period for the studio. Long known for making low-budget horror films and monster movies, the studio began to evolve into an entertainment powerhouse on several fronts. First, it began investing in television and was one of the few major studios to see the opportunities there.

The oldest movie studio in the United States, Universal saw a major takeover by MCA that began in the mid-1950s. As the days of actors under studio contracts came to an end, talent agencies like MCA found new strength in the system and began creating opportunities for their performers by packaging studio projects. Soon they began financially backing studios like Universal. As the decade wore on they saw an opportunity to create an entertainment empire through television, the roster of talent and production studio's lots, sets, costumes, crews and film technology helped pull it all together. By the dawn of the 60s, MCA had taken over Universal. Stars like Lana Turner who aligned themselves with shrewd agents, good projects and powerful studios saw the benefit through their film opportunities. *The Lady Takes a Flyer*, some say, was a "sharply packaged audience-pleaser" that was the "perfect example of the satisfying-yet-disposable Universal product of that era."

In June 1957, Universal's lot suffered a major fire, destroying its New York street film studio set. The cause was believed to be arson, and the fire damaged a half a million dollars worth of valuable studio property. It also impacted the number and type of films Universal could make that year. One of the reasons *The Lady Takes a Flyer* was able to meet it's production schedule was because the film consisted almost entirely of interior studio filming with the only external footage being of airstrips and runways. It was one of the few films that didn't require the burned out lot.

Universal's leading man, Jeff Chandler, was teamed with Lana Turner and the pair made a striking couple on the screen. While Turner's stardom shined far brighter than Chandler's, he was still one of the studio's most popular male stars of the 50s. Starting his career in radio, he made his first film for Universal in 1949 called *Abandoned.* As the decade progressed, his roles grew bigger and the films more successful. His prematurely gray hair, mixed with his hand-

Lana with Jeff Chandler in a publicity shot for *The Lady Takes a Flyer.*

some, strong looks made him a strong match for major leading ladies. He would find himself paired with most of the major actresses of the day, including Joan Crawford, June Allyson, Kim Novak, Jayne Russell, Esther Williams, Maureen O'Hara, Susan Hayward and others.

With direction from Jack Arnold, the actors and special effects were married with beautiful interiors from art director Alexander Golitzen. The film was produced by William Alland, who had collaborated with Arnold on a string of sci-fi films like *Creature from the Black Lagoon* and *It Came from Outer Space*.

The New York Times found the film "surprisingly ingratiating" while the *New York Daily News* called it "pleasing." For Lana, the picture was a welcome one, allowing her to show that she wasn't washed up and still had some strong performances in good pictures to deliver. MGM wasn't the only studio that could benefit from her beauty and popularity, and she could still make a living after 20 years in Hollywood.

By the time of *The Lady Takes a Flyer,* Lana was once again single after the failure of her marriage to Lex Barker. After Lana miscarried in 1956, she underwent a hysterectomy.

Her hopes of having another child ended and the marriage came crashing down after her only daughter Cheryl told Lana's mother that Barker had been molesting her. After her mother disclosed the news to Lana, she immediately kicked him out and ended things. Some stories suggest she held a gun to his head while he was sleeping and considered killing him, but decided he wasn't worth spending the remainder of her life in jail; so, she simply filed for divorce. Barker told Lana, "Whatever your daughter told you, it's a lie." Lana failed to believe him.

During the filming of *Lady Takes a Flyer*, Lana began receiving phone calls from a man who identified himself as Mr. John Steele. Initially, she refused to take the calls; because she had no idea who the man was and it was not unusual for Lana to find herself the subject of attention from strangers who felt they knew her after having seen her in the movies.

Steele continued to call, attempting to get her on the line. "I left word that I wouldn't accept his calls," recalled Lana. "But even though they were headed off at the switchboard, the calls kept coming."

One day Steele called the studio while Lana was with her make-up man and longtime friend Del Armstrong. Lana asked Del if he would call the man back and find out exactly who he was and what he wanted. Armstrong agreed and returned to tell Lana, "All he wants is to send you some flowers. I told him there wouldn't be anything wrong with that," Armstrong told Lana.

The next day a bouquet of flowers arrived at the studio. Soon more flower bouquets began arriving day after day. "There were so many of them that they wouldn't fit into my dressing room," wrote the star in her autobiography. "And what magnificent flowers – a vast variety of them, as luxuriant as they were profuse. There was a card, of course, with just the name – John Steele – and a phone number. Now, I was intrigued and certainly I was flattered."

Several days later, Lana called the number on the card to thank John Steele for his attention. "The flowers are overwhelming, but do I know you, Mr. Steele? Have we met?", asked Lana.

In what she found to be a pleasantly masculine voice he told her that they had never met, but that he had admired her for a long time and that he knew a friend of hers, Ava Gardner.

It would later be discovered that John Steele was better known as Johnny Stompanato, a small-time associate of LA organized crime man Mickey Cohen. Stompanato had reportedly tried to meet and romance a number of Hollywood's leading ladies including Ava Gardner and Janet Leigh, but none would ever succumb to his ploys or refer to him as a friend. Not until Lana Turner.

Lana believed that if Steele had been acquainted with Ava

Gardner, it was a good sign that he was legitimate, but she was still suspicious of his attention. When he invited her to dinner she replied that she never went out while she was working. When he persisted, asking her to go out to dinner with him some weekend when she wasn't working she told him that her weekends were spent with her mother and daughter. He then asked if she'd be open to lunch, or even just a drink. She refused, but said she'd call if she found herself free.

Steele continued to pursue her, Lana recollected. More flowers arrived the next day, followed by record albums of music she enjoyed. She liked the attention but wondered about how he knew what sort of music she enjoyed. She later learned that he managed to find someone on the set that confided in him the music the star enjoyed. "He had mysterious ways of obtaining information and had access, as I was to learn to my bitter cost," she said.

The flowers, music and calls kept coming and finally she broke, calling him and agreeing to a drink with him. "I'll tell you what," she said to Steele. "I'll be working late here, but if you'd like to stop by for a drink after I get home, I might be able to see you for a little while. But call first," It was a moment she'd come to regret.

By the time *The Lady Takes a Flyer* was released, Lana was be deep in the throws of a tumultuous relationship with Johnny Stompanato. She was also be back at the top of Hollywood's A-list celebrities, nominated for an Academy Award for Best Actress. In fact, in promotional material for the movie release the studio heralded, "New Excitement for Luscious Lana, "Best Actress" Academy Nominee for her role in *Peyton Place*."

FIVE

"A gentleman is simply a patient wolf."
- Lana Turner

In fiction, John Steele was an American soldier serving during the Civil War, World War I and World War II. Through unknown means, he possesses super-human strength. According to Marvel Comics Universe, he would become "America's real first Super-Soldier" making Steele the predecessor of Captain America. In real life it was a name used by an LA gangster by the name of Johnny Stompanato. Whether he chose the name because of its fictional origins may never be known.

A DARK FIGURE ENTERS HER LIFE

"And that's how the blackest period in my life began," said Lana Turner, looking back at her entanglement with John Steele, aka Johnny Stompanato, and her decision to give him her private phone number. She would lose much more to the man before it was over, but initially she found him charismatic and handsome. "I believed the lies a man told me," she recalled. "And by the time I learned they were lies it was too late. I was trapped, helpless because of my fear for my own life, for Cheryl's, and my mother's."

It was mid-May 1957, recalled Turner. "In those days I drove a big gray Cadillac I called the Baby Whale. After I pulled it into my usual spot outside the apartment house. and went to get my script from the backseat, I happened to glance across the street, where a streetlight shone onto a parked car. It was a black Lincoln Continental, with a man sitting inside. I saw him get out and begin walking in my direction. That seemed a bit strange and I shivered as I hurried to the elevator and pressed the button."

Moments after she got into her apartment there was a knock at her door. The maid answered and told the stranger to wait. Locating Lana in the bedroom her maid told her a man identifying himself only as Mr. Steele was there to see her. "But he was supposed to telephone?" she pondered aloud and then asked Arminda, her housekeeper, what he looked like. "A nice looking man," she replied.

"Well, show him into the living room," Lana replied. After

Johnny with Lana in happier times in 1957.

settling herself and checking her appearance in the mirror, she entered the living room to find a tall, husky, dark-haired man who she thought to be "around my own age," standing before her.

While Lana was introduced to this handsome stranger as "John Steele," he was known to others as a variety of other names, including "Handsome Harry," "Johnny Stomp," "Johnny Valentine," and even "Oscar" – because rumors around Hollywood suggested his penis was as big as an Academy Award. He was a former United States Marine whose main claim to fame, at the time, was as an associate of Los Angeles gangster Mickey Cohen. Cohen was sent to Los Angeles by East Coast mobsters to keep an eye on Bugsy Siegel, but he was instrumental in setting up the Flamingo Hotel in Las Vegas as a sports booking operation, along with other Vegas betting enterprises.

Cohen hired the five-foot-eleven, 180-pound John Stompanato as a bodyguard and sometimes enforcer in his local LA business undertakings, but Stompanato's path west started on the straight and narrow, with the best of intentions.

Born into an Italian-American family in Woodstock, Illinois, on October 10, 1925, John Stompanato, Jr. was the son of John Sr., owner of a small barbershop. His mother, Carmela, was a seamstress, and both were first generation immigrants from in Italy. They married in Brooklyn and relocated to Woodstock around 1916. The youngest of four children, Johnny had two sisters; Grace and Teresa, as well as an older brother, Carmine. Less than a week after his birth, his mother died of peritonitis. His father would remarry and Johnny, as the youngest son, would have the full attention of his sisters and stepmother growing up.

In 1940 he was sent to Kemper Military School for boys in Boonville, Missouri, to instill discipline and prepare him for the future. With World War II growing closer to U.S. soil, it was certain John Jr. would end up in the fight. After graduating at the age 17,

John joined the Marines in 1943. He saw action in the South West Pacific Theatre, in the Battle of Peleliu and in Okinawa, and reportedly found himself stationed in China in 1945.

After his military service ended in 1946, he married a Turkish girl named Sarah Utish, who he had met while stationed in Tianjin, China. The couple settled in Stompanato's hometown of Woodstock, a small town about 90 miles northwest of Chicago. There they had son, John III. The marriage fell apart and ended in divorce after his wife walked out on him. Stompanato soon grew restless and left Woodstock for Los Angeles seeking fortune. He worked in a pet shop and spent time as an auto salesman. When things didn't pan out he took a job as a bouncer at one of Mickey Cohen's nightclubs. Soon he was doing more for Cohen and with the increased responsibility came a chance to make more money. In addition to the role of part-time bodyguard, Stompanato sometimes acted as Cohen's money-man, earning about $300 a week. Twice he was arrested after police found him carrying more than $50,000 in cash. It was common for the syndicate to employ low-level hoods to carry the money because they were less likely to be arrested and searched. He was again arrested on suspicion of armed robbery in 1952, but police were unable to make the charges stick.

Stompanato was also described as a gigolo. When he wasn't doing Cohen's dirty work he was often found with his arm around a beautiful, sometimes, older woman. Older women appealed to him because they often had money to spend on him.

In Los Angeles, Stompanato "officially" made his living as the owner and manager of The Myrtlewood Gift Shop in Westwood, California. Selling inexpensive pottery and carved wood sculptures, he presented himself as a collector and seller of fine art, but Stompanato reportedly spent very little time in the shop and found most of his income coming from his work for Cohen. He even had business trips to Sweden, Brussels, Uruguay and Brazil that were passed off as antiques business, but some suspected they too were mob related.

In LA, Stompanato tied the knot several times before meeting Lana. He married actress Helen Gilbert in 1948, who was best known for supporting roles in films like *The Secret of Dr. Kildare* in 1939 and *The Isle of Missing Men* in 1942. During divorce proceedings she testified in court that, "Johnny had no means. I did what I could to support him." The police took Johnny for a gigolo and reportedly made a note of it in the dossier they kept on him writing, "When the victim's money is dissipated, he becomes interested in another woman. Usually he frequents expensive nightspots to meet wealthy female types."

In 1950 he had eyes on Janet Leigh. Leigh was at the early stages of her career, still living at home with her parents when she began receiving bouquets of flowers accompanied by Billy Eckstine records, arriving daily at her home with cards signed, 'Johnny.'

Eventually, the flowers resulted in a phone call. "No — you don't know me," said the caller "But I know and admire you and would like to take you out."

Leigh recalled that the voice was deep and masculine, and while she was intrigued she told him she wouldn't go out on a date with a total stranger, but he was welcome to meet her provided she was accompanied by her parents. She recalled that he arrived sharply, at 6 p.m., and was a "tall, powerfully built, dark-haired, extremely handsome man who had just parked a Cadillac in the driveway."

"I'm Johnny," he announced and then along with Janet and her parents he engaged in pleasant and polite conversation. He would only describe himself as a "businessman" said Leigh.

Leigh eventually did agree to a date, with Stompanato taking her to a private club near the Pacific Coast Highway, just south of Malibu. It was here he disclosed more about his work. "Janet, I am going to tell you something now — something about me — that is highly confidential. I must trust you with this, because I want you to be 'my girl."

"I am a syndicate man, a member of the mob," she recalled him saying. "This lounge is frequented only by those on the inside who are in the know and in good standing. When one of us takes a girl, he has to be sure of her loyalty…my name is Johnny Stompanato."

Leigh said she was "flabbergasted" at what he had told her and she responded by saying that while she assured him "their conversation was indeed confidential," she just couldn't handle his profession. She said Stompanato took her home and she never heard from him again. But his interest in starlets and leading ladies would continue.

He would marry again briefly in 1953 to a young Hollywood actress names Helen Stanley, a 24-year-old starlet at Twentieth-Century Fox. He placed himself in the role of her agent and tried to get her into the spotlight, but the plans didn't work and the couple would divorce the same year.

Lana reportedly knew he had been married and had a son, but wasn't aware to the full extent of Stompanato's way with the ladies or his gangland activities. He preferred to keep it that way. Even if Lana wasn't aware of John Steele's activities, the Los Angeles Police Department (LAPD) was. After numerous arrests, sources in the LAPD claimed they were well aware of Stompanato's association with Cohen and detectives in the "Gangster Squad" had a standing rule that if they ever saw Cohen or Stompanato they were to immediately put them under surveillance. Police didn't want any mob wars within city limits, so the duo, as well as their associates, were often tailed wherever they went.

More than a few of the LAPD's Gangster Squad enjoyed harassing Stompanato when the opportunity arose. Former LAPD cop Fred Otash said at one time the cops were frustrated after Stompanto had pulled a caper in town and they were unable to get anything on him. They spotted him driving down the Sunset Strip and decide to "have some fun."

Otash told his partner to pull up alongside Stompanato's car slowly. "I unlocked our shotgun and pulled it out of the bracket. When we were parallel to Stompanato, I stuck the barrel of the gun out the

A man of many names, Johnny Stompanato passed himself off as a shop owner by day, and a sometimes runner or bodyguard for LA mobster Mickey Cohen by night.

window and shouted to Johnny, 'Now you've had it, you mother-fucker.' When Johnny saw the shotgun, he ducked, losing control of his new Cadillac. It went over the curb and down over the hill of Sunset. He could have been killed."

All Lana knew of the new man in her life was that he dated Ava Gardner, and even that was a bit of a stretch. No romance between the two was ever reported and Stompanato even admitted as much. After a drink with Lana he asked if he might see her again. She said it was possible, only if he phoned in advance. She didn't like people showing up on her doorstep without notice.

She originally told people, "I didn't know him, but we had mutual friends. We went on a blind date. He kept calling me after that, and would come over for a drink or a chat."

More flowers arrived and John Steele called, asking Lana for a date. She suggested lunch at her apartment, not wanting to be seen in public with a man she didn't know yet. He offered to bring lunch, arriving on time with vermicelli with clam sauce from her favorite restaurant. She was initially impressed with the fact that he managed to bring her favorite meal for their first lunch, but later wished she had seen it as a warning flag that he had become too aware of her habits and interests in such a short time.

Over lunch that day he gave her a gift – it was a bracelet of small gold leaves inset with diamonds and engraved with her initials. She said she couldn't accept such a gift so soon after meeting him, but he insisted since he'd had it engraved and could no longer return it. Lana would accept his gift and return the favor later by presenting him with a gold charm bracelet engraved with, "For Johnny ... Sweet Love ... When you wear this, remember it is a tiny piece of my heart ... and also remember, be careful ... With all my soul, Lanita."

She claimed he was not very forthcoming about explaining what he did for a living, but somehow she got the impression from the things he did say that he had something to do with producing records. She felt he always managed to change the subject or avoid answering any questions about his background and she was too caught up in the initial romance to care. "He clearly knew how to court a woman," she said. "He had the kind of dark good looks that always attracted me, and his attentiveness soothed the hurt of those last grim months with Lex." Lana's marriage to Lex Barker, her last husband, had ended badly and Lana had avoided romantic entanglements for some time after the divorce, focusing her attention on her mother Mildred and daughter Cheryl.

Cheryl Crane was 13 at the time and entering those difficult teenage years. She spent time shuffling between boarding school, her grandmother, and her father, Stephen Crane, as well as Lana. Cheryl, at the time, had been moved into her grandmother's guest room as Lana's leased home on Mapleton Drive was pending sale and all the contents put in storage. Lana had moved into a penthouse on Wilshire Boulevard. Lana's divorce became final in July and she would claim Johnny would become more possessive after that, hoping they might marry.

As a glamorous movie star, Lana was still in her 30s and found it difficult to imagine herself as the mother of a teenage daughter. It certainly didn't help her image as a movie goddess, as starlets like Marilyn Monroe were filling the publicity magazines the way Lana used to, and good scripts were becoming hard to come by.

However, in 1957 a part came her way that she couldn't refuse, but it was one that was coming a bit close to home. Could she tackle the role of a mother with a teenage daughter? While it certainly was a role she was familiar with, what would it do to her movie goddess image?

Six

All men are alike. The approach is different; the result is always the same."

- Lana Turner as Constance McKenzie in 'Peyton Place' 1957

With her career on the rocks, Lana landed a film role that would earn her an Oscar nomination and tell the critics she was far from washed up. But the career boost would be overshadowed by the darkness of her troubled romance.

PEYTON PLACE

Lana Turner, according to her daughter, was not fully equipped with the best of instincts when it came to motherhood. "Mother was not one to get herself involved in diapers and feedings," Cheryl Crane said of her early childhood with her mother.

After the divorce from Stephen Crane, Cheryl was raised mostly by nannies, and by her maternal grandmother, Mildred. "Nana was the only one who hugged me, usually on Thursdays," she said. "On mother's strict orders, I was never ever to be left alone, not even in my room. Nana tended to me 24-hours a day, except for Thursdays and every other Sunday, when Gran came in."

Initially MGM feared motherhood might spell doom for their leading sex symbol, but it didn't quite turn out that way. Her fan mail reportedly jumped the year after Cheryl's birth, tying Lana

with Judy Garland for the most fan mail in a nine-month period. In addition to her vast collection of male fans, Lana would find herself gaining a multitude of female fans who admired her for appearing to have it all.

Though Lana called her daughter "Baby" until she was 14, Lana didn't really know what to do with a young child, and as Cheryl aged, things didn't seem to get any better. Cheryl felt as if the Hollywood system left her mother with a selfishness that made her unable to give of herself the way a mother would for her child. While there was a bond between the two, Lana's mothering instinct was more about appearing proper, pretty and well behaved, most of all for Cheryl, it was not to embarrass or make her mother look bad.

Cheryl reportedly was molested by Lana's fifth husband, Lex Barker, best known as the man who inherited the role of *Tarzan* from Johnny Weissmuller. When Lana found out, she kicked Barker out, but struggled to find a way to deal with her daughter. When Cheryl ran away at the age of 13, Lana's first words when she came to collect her at the police station were, "Thank god you're safe," but they were quickly followed by, "How could you do this to me?"

Two weeks after collecting her runaway, Lana was offered a new role. It was quite a change of pace from the goddesses, femme fatales and screen sirens she was used to playing. In fact, it was actually much closer to reality than she might have enjoyed. It was the role of a mother of a troubled teenage daughter. The film was *Peyton Place*.

Directed by Mark Robson, the screenplay for *Peyton Place* came from John Michael Hayes. Grace Metalious, author of the novel on which the film was based, served as a "story consultant", but reportedly brought little to transferring the tale from book to screen.

The 1956 novel would be a best seller upon its release. So much so that Twentieth-Century Fox producer Jerry Wald paid the author $250,000 for the film rights less than a month after the book was published. One of the challenges the film faced was in presenting the low morals and tawdry aspects of the story on the big screen.

An exposé of the lives and loves of residents of a small New England mill town called Peyton Place, the book comes complete with scandal, homicide, suicide, incest, and a healthy dose of sex mired with often misguided morality.

The story is told through the narration of Allison MacKenzie, a high school senior who has aspirations of being an author and uses her town and her neighbors as the characters for a book. She wants nothing more than to escape the repressed town and explore the world. At the same time, her best friend is struggling with an abusive stepfather and her other high school pals are working through their own host of issues of figuring out who they are, what their parents expect them to be, and ultimately what will become of them.

In the feature, Lana plays Constance MacKenzie, mother of Allison who presents herself as a prim and proper woman that in real-

Russ Tamblin, Lana Turner and Diane Varsi in a scene from 'Peyton Place.

ity is a sexually repressed hypocrite who had an affair with a married businessman and gave birth to his child out of wedlock. She hides the secret from her daughter and the entire town.

Producer Jerry Wald reportedly never intended or wanted Metalious to contribute anything to the film, but used the author as an opportunity to increase publicity for the film. She reportedly grew disenchanted with the story changes and left the production to return home. Although she hated the resulting feature film, the success of *Peyton Place* the movie would make the author a wealthy woman. She would earn $400,000 in profits from the successful release.

Screenwriter John Michael Hayes struggled with the studio and the Hollywood morality office, known as the Hays Code, as he attempted to translate the sexuality and drama of the book into a feature film onto the big screen. Producer Jerry Wald knew if they could get enough of the story on screen and capitalize on the book's success, he had a surefire hit on his hands. And Wald knew a thing or two about hits.

Between the 1930s and 1960s, Jerry Wald had his handprint on some of Hollywood's biggest films. By the time *Peyton Place* had come along, he was one of the most powerful men at Twentieth-Century Fox, if not all of Hollywood. He had controlled the destinies of more than a few stars of Tinseltown.

Wald's films included *Stars Over Broadway* (1935), *The Roaring Twenties* (1939), *They Drive by Night* (1940), *Navy Blues* (1941), *Across the Pacific* (1942), *The Man Who Came to Dinner* (1942), *Destination Tokyo* (1943), *Johnny Belinda* (1948), *Key Largo* (1948), *The Glass Menagerie* (1950), *Perfect Strangers* (1950), *Two Tickets to Broadway* (1951), *The Blue Veil* (1951), and *An Affair to Remember* (1957), among others.

Jerry Wald was also the mastermind behind Joan Crawford's career resurgence after her being dropped by MGM. She would turn up at Warner Bros. with her Academy Award winning performance in *Mildred Pierce* in 1945. Now, it was Lana's chance to recover, and it was Wald who set the plans in motion.

Without any prospects of work after completing *The Lady*

Lana Turner and Hope Lange both earned Oscar nominations for their performances.

Takes a Flyer, Lana had planned to spend time with Cheryl but in the spring of 1957, Wald called her just as she was finishing up at Universal and offered her the role of Constance MacKenzie. It was tough enough for Lana to accept herself as the mother of a troubled teen in real life, but to try to convince her fans of it might shatter the glossy image she had created in more than 20 years on screen. But "the script was too tempting to turn down," she said.

Lana accepted the part and proved to be a wise move. The publicity alone put her back in the gossip columns and had everyone talking. Louella Parsons broke the news on April 15, 1957, when she told the world "Luscious Lana signs to play mother role!"

The real question on everyone's mind was how would her fans react. Few of her contemporaries - and many leading ladies who were older than she - refused to tackle mother roles for fear of it destroying their careers. When Parson's broke the news she wrote Lana was "intrigued with the idea of playing the mother of a girl of 18," and that it was "going to be such a big picture, she'd be foolish not to accept it pronto."

Sharing the screen with Lana was Hope Lange, Diane Varsi, Lloyd Nolan, Russ Tamblyn, Terry Moore, Barry Coe, and a host of other competent actors.

The film was shot primarily in Camden, Maine, but some exteriors were also shot in nearby towns of Belfast and Rockland as well as in Lake Placid, New York. However, Lana refused to travel for location shooting so a stand-in was used for the shots at a distance and all other work taking place on Hollywood soundstages on the Fox lot. Lana claimed that during several of the scenes, she is seen wearing jewelry gifts given to her by her new suitor, John Steele. She'd claim that years later, seeing those scenes when the film aired on television would give her chills.

Peyton Place premiered in Camden, where much of the exteriors were shot, two days before its general U.S. release on December 13, 1957. It was rushed into release in hopes of garnering Academy Award nominations for the 1957 awards ceremony and targeting the Christmas holiday.

Peyton Place was one of the highest grossing films of 1957, alongside *Bridge on the River Kwai* and *Old Yeller,* but because it arrived at Christmas, much of its ticket sales spilled into 1958. It earned upwards of $16 million ($135 million in 2014 dollars) at the box office. While much of the interest came from the fact that it was based on a steamy best seller, the tragedy involving Lana and Johnny Stompanato would help boost ticket sales, because the troubles off the screen were as salacious as those detailed in the film, if not more. By the time of the tragedy *Peyton Place's* run in America's theaters was all but done, but new interest drew moviegoers back to the film. The film saw box office receipts reportedly jump by a third the week after the Stompanato killing.

While *Peyton Place* was both a critical and commercial success many felt that too many of the darkest elements of the novel were stripped down or eliminated completely by the film version. In *The New York Times*, Bosley Crowther remarked, "There is no sense of massive corruption here."

Variety wrote, "In leaning backwards not to offend, producer and writer have gone acrobatic. On the screen is not the unpleasant sex-secret little town against which Grace Metalious set her story. These aren't the gossiping, spiteful, immoral people she portrayed. There are hints of this in the film, but only hints."

Stanley Kauffman of the *Saturday Review* gave Lana high marks writing, "Lana Turner, given a chance with a role of some depth, proves that she can be as persuasive as some of the Method-dedicated girls flocking into movies these days."

The film garnered nine Academy Award nominations, in-cluding a Best Actress nomination for Lana and three other acting nominations. However, the film would tie the Academy's record for biggest shutout. *The Little Foxes* also had nine nominations and no wins a number of years earlier - a record that has since been broken.

In addition to Lana's Best Actress nomination, the film

received nominations for Best Picture, Best Director, Best Supporting Actress nominations for both Diane Varsi and Hope Lange, Best Supporting Actor nominations Arthur Kennedy and Russ Tamblyn and nominations for Best Adapted Screenplay and Best Cinematography.

Lana would hear from Jerry Wald months later after the film's release in hopes of a follow up project. During her vacation in Acapulco, Wald reportedly called Lana numerous times hoping to convince her to play a southern belle in a film called *The Sound and the Fury,* but Lana rejected the offer not wanting to play an older woman in the film.

SEVEN

"The thing about happiness is that it doesn't help you to grow; only unhappiness does that. So I'm grateful that my bed of roses was made up equally of blossoms and thorns. I've had a privileged, creative, exciting life, and I think that the parts that were less joyous were preparing me, testing me, strengthening me."

- Lana Turner

With a mixture of excitement, danger, mystery - and even romance - Lana finds herself falling deeper and deeper under the control of Johnny Stompanato.

Doomed Romance

As a lover, Lana found John Steele to be "considerate and gentle." He was very elusive about what he did for a living but, "he didn't speak like anyone associated with a mobster."

Later she would look back trying to find clues to who he really was and how long it was before she realized this romance spelled danger and tragedy. "He told me that he had been married and had a son," she recalled. "Although he looked younger, he said he was 39. And I couldn't believe he would just lie about his name."

She introduced him to her mother and daughter while *Peyton Place* was in production. One day at her apartment, when the pair were getting a tour of her new Wilshire penthouse, Lana told Cheryl, "Mother has met a very nice gentleman … His name is John Stompanato, and he's got a horse."

Cheryl loved horses and Lana explained that one afternoon they'd manage a trip out to the stables so she could see the horse.

Lana admitted that during the filming of *Peyton Place* she finally learned who John Steele really was. "One day a friend of mine - I won't tell you his name – came to see me, with something on his mind. He just blurted it out, 'Lana, you can tell me to go to hell, but for your own good there is something you should know. It's about your friend.'"

"Well, what is it?" Lana inquired.

"You're seeing a man whose real name is Johnny Stompanato," her friend replied.

"But, that's impossible. He wouldn't lie to me. We care for each other."

She learned the flowers that John Steele had been sending her were coming from a flower shop owned by Mickey Cohen. She was aware of Cohen by reputation. Later, when she confided in her friend Del Armstrong about who she was really dating, he had heard of him as well.

When she got up the courage to confront her new boyfriend, he told her, "I've always told you the truth."

When she pressed him as to why he was going by the name John Steele, he explained that he had been using the name John Steele for years. When she told him she had heard his real name was Johnny Stompanato, "a dark red color came into his dark cheeks."

He told her he knew that if he had been truthful with her about his association with Cohen, at the beginning, she never would have agreed to go out with him.

"I think we'd better not see each other anymore," Lana

responded.

"Lana, darling, just try and get away from me," he told her, laughing in her face.

"He made gangster threats," Cheryl said. "You can't get away from me. You'll never get away from me," she recalled hearing him tell her mother.

Lana didn't realize it at the time, but she would come to realize getting away from Johnny Stompanato would be a lot more

difficult than she imagined. She claimed that she began going out with other men to be seen in the company of more reputable men, but Stompanato kept calling. She eventually started hanging up on him and one night he managed to get into her apartment by climbing onto the fire escape and getting through the locked back door.

Lana says she awoke to a man coming through her bedroom door. He immediately pounced onto the bed, straddling her with his arms pinned at her sides and his weight upon her. She was unable to move. She said her face was at first covered with a pillow and just before she was to black out he removed it. "I shrieked at him while he tried to kiss me, using every foul word I could think of. "Get the hell out of here, or I'm calling the police."

She admitted – and Stompanato knew it – she had no intention of calling the police. The last thing Lana wanted was bad publicity from her association with a gangster. More than that, she also found "his consuming passion was strangely exciting."

She admitted in her autobiography that the "attraction was very deep – maybe something sick within me – and my dangerous captivation went far beyond lovemaking. In fact, the sex was nothing special."

Lana felt that some theorized her attraction to dangerous men came from the fact that her father was a gambler and that he had been murdered. Perhaps, somehow the danger added a level of excitement that her subconscious desired. She was never convinced that's what it was.

Stompanato forced his way back into Lana's life and into her bed. She then said that he began to become more threatening, showing signs of the man she feared he might be. She claimed he "took pains to remind me that he had the power to harm me and my family."

She said his threats were vague at first, but began to evolve from general threats to promises that he rather her be dead than to let her go. In time they became more specific, like disfiguring her by cutting up her face, so she could never work again, or killing her daughter or mother.

Though Lana claimed she feared for her life, she also avoided seeking help, if not for herself, but for her mother and child. She was drawn to this man and his power over her and the fear it created

was strong and alluring. As much as Lana claimed she tried to keep him away, she continued to reach for him. "Sometimes mother called him five times in a half hour," recalled Cheryl.

Cheryl said that although people often spread rumors that there was some romantic interest between the two of them, it was never true. "He bent over backward to make sure our friendship was never misunderstood," she said.

Cheryl remembered that while riding the horse Johnny had offered her, a friend of her father's saw the two of them together and commented to Stephen Crane that Stompanato had been seen with his hands on his daughter, helping her on and off the horse. Cheryl's father would have only one meeting and conversation with John Stompanato, telling him only, "My daughter's the most important thing in the world to me, and I do care what happens to her."

While the relationship and exchanges between Cheryl and Johnny were relatively benign, the relationship between Johnny and Lana became more volatile as it evolved. "Awful fights, screaming and yelling and smashing glasses and just, you know, things I wasn't used to hearing," said Cheryl.

Cheryl was quoted at the time as saying that she believed Johnny's only real intentions with her were to use her to get to her mother. "He used to take me on little trips, to the market, ice cream parlors, and shops. He tried to use me to promote marriage between him and my mother."

Lana claimed that when things were at their bleakest, she saw an escape hatch open when a movie role came along that would take her to London for months and allow her to escape this dangerous man. Though on some level Lana may have wanted an escape, on another level, she found that she didn't want to escape. She was playing with fire.

EIGHT

"[He said] he would get me where it would hurt the most, and that would be my daughter and my mother."
- Lana Turner

From major roles onscreen and worldwide attention off-screen, she lived a life far more exciting and dramatic than most of the movies she'd ever appear in.

ANOTHER TIME, ANOTHER PLACE

While Lana claimed she longed for an "escape" from the lover Stompanato, in reality it was not as simple as that. It wasn't only that Stompanato was determined to hold onto his leading lady, but also that Lana wasn't quite ready to let go.

Lana was exactly the sort of woman Stompanato found himself attracted to – beautiful, older … and wealthy. By the summer of 1957, Lana was aware of his real name and was already writing checks made out to "John Stompanato Steele." Her suitor was only

too happy to have wealthy women fund his way of life, and he'd
been doing it for some time. He also liked the idea of dating a movie
star. If not Ava Garner or Janet Leigh, Lana Turner would most
certainly do.

As for Lana, she was attracted to the man and the power he
held over her. While she claimed the sex was nothing special, during
a trip to Acapulco, guests found it hard not to hear the loud lovemaking coming from their cabana. Lana always enjoyed having a man
take care of things for her and enjoyed having a man on her arm at
most times. If he were a strong, handsome and powerful man, all the
better.

What Lana was unaware of was the fact that Johnny was
actually five years her junior. He lied, telling her he was older than
she was. Lana believed she'd found a tall, dark, handsome, masculine man who had power – and maybe a little danger – and she found
that attractive.

Most of her husbands and lovers fit the bill in one way
or another. Stompanato, however, had more of an edge, and more
danger than she bargained for, including his association with local

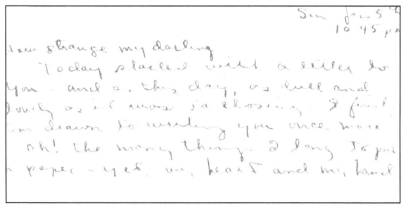

Written in January 1958, Lana was still reaching out to Stompanato. "Today started with a letter to you," she wrote. "and as
this day, as dull and lonely as it was, closes, I find I'm drawn to
writing you once more.

mobsters. Once Lana knew who he was, he made it no secret that he was capable of causing trouble. When she made him angry, he was only too happy to tell Lana she could easily find herself on the wrong side of that trouble.

Leaving for London for a film gave her an excuse to get away from Stompanato, but she continued to see him up until the time she left, and they corresponded regularly after she embarked on her journey. Lana didn't actually accept the film in order to escape Johnny. She needed the work. With few offers coming in, it was important to her career to stay active on the big screen.

In accepting the film she negotiated a role as co-producer on the film. This new role gave Lana had the ability to approve the selection of her co-stars that included Barry Sullivan and Glynis Johns. *Another Time, Another Place* would also mark the first major film introducing Sean Connery to moviegoers. While Connery had several smaller roles on television and uncredited or bit parts in film, he is "introduced" to the world in the credits of this film and would go onto fame and fortune as James Bond and a host of other roles. At 27 years old, he was nearly a decade younger than Lana and only about five years younger than Johnny Stompanato. Because it was a Paramount Release, Sean Connery had to be loaned out to the production by Twentieth-Century Fox. It would be the first widely distributed film in the U.S. featuring Connery in a major role.

Paramount was able to get Lana signed to the film at a salary below her standard, because she was no longer signed to MGM and was in need of work. The opportunity to co-produce the film would help her if the film did well. *Another Time, Another Place* tells the tale of an American reporter, Sara Scott, played by Lana, who is on assignment in Europe during World War II. She finds herself in an affair with a British reporter named Mark Trevor, played by Sean Connery. At the same time, she is fending off the affections of her old boss and finding herself faced with making a decision to either marry her rich boss or her handsome reporter boyfriend. After choosing the younger man, she is crushed to discover that not only is he married, he also has a son. The two struggle with how to work out their complicated relationship.

As the war ends, Mark is killed in an accident. Her boss convinces her it is time to come back to the United States, however, before she goes, she visits Mark's hometown, meeting her ex-lover's wife and child and finding closure in the experience.

It was a fairly typical feature for Lana, with her playing a young and beautiful woman caught up in a tragic love affair; surrounded by exciting locations and looking as glamorous as possible as she fought back tears brought on by the tragedies of the script.

Principal photography for the black and white film began in September 1957 in a small village in Cornwall called Palperro. Located in the southwest peninsula of Great Britain, the area is known for its cold, damp and often dreary weather. The town would serve as the hometown of Connery's character in the film. While Connery was a relative newcomer to the big screen, he found the production a bit of a disappointment. "The script was not entirely satisfactory," he would say. "They were rewriting as they were shooting, so they started with the end first, and I was dead at the end … so by the time they led up to me, I was only a picture on a piano. The film wasn't very good. It was beautifully lit but dreadfully directed."

Connery escorted Lana to various events, much to the dismay of her current boyfriend. Stompanato began to suspect the two were having an affair. Sean Connery has said little of the filming or his association with Lana, except to say Lana was "a lovely lady."

Filming carried on through the fall and into winter. For Lana, it became a lonely period, away from her family and friends. Aside from her make-up man, Del Armstrong, she had no real friends when she arrived in London. Armstrong almost didn't make it either. Since the unions wouldn't allow the film company to employ an American on the set to do Lana's make-up, she managed to have him promoted to an assistant producer, so that she could bring him along. Armstrong would arrive at her rented home in Hampstead each morning to help her apply her fake eyebrows. Early in Lana's career, the studio shaved off her eyebrows to draw them in for a better visual for the camera, but her natural ones never grew back. Armstrong would help her use fake eyebrows for years after and became a trusted friend in the process.

As the dreary weather continued and all Lana did was work, she found herself exchanging letters with Johnny back home. Regularly arriving letters of love and longing had Lana, believing she had left something special behind, and she began to miss it. She even found herself writing back to him sharing her deep feelings for this man she claimed she feared. Calling him "Daddy" or "Papite" and referring to herself as "Little Lana," she wrote, "I adore the way you write and all the truly beautiful things you say to me – so please, please dearest continue. Every line warms me and makes me ache and miss you more each tiny moment. It's true – it's beautiful, but terrible. But, just so is deep love ... we are truly in tune 'all the way' ... Know how dearly I love you angel ... hold me dear lover mi macho."

Her loneliness finally drove her to pay for a ticket to fly Johnny to London to be with her for the duration of the filming. Lana and Johnny once again picked up their love affair, far away from Hollywood, but soon Stompanato, she claimed, began to grow more possessive of her and suspicious of every moment she spent away from him.

With Lana working full time on the film, Johnny quickly became bored hanging about by himself. He convinced Lana to let him keep her company on the set, but once he got a good look at her co-star, he grew more concerned that her affection for her leading man might be more than just acting. His jealousy caused him to become even more unpleasant and controlling. She began to fear he actually might hurt her.

It was suggested that while in England Johnny became physically violent again with Lana. Bored and complaining constantly about Lana's refusals to be seen in public with him one evening, their argument escalated into a shoving match. "I reached for the phone, but he knocked it away and lunged for my throat," Lana recalled. "As his grip closed around my larynx, I managed to let out a loud scream, though I could feel the strain on my vocal chords."

Lana found work as a way to escape Johnny, but he was waiting for her at the end of every evening. "Underlying everything was my shame," Lana said. "I was so ashamed. I didn't want anybody to know my predicament, how foolish I'd been, how I'd taken him at face value and been completely duped."

Stompanato, she claimed, was incredibly jealous, and had heard rumors in gossip columns that Lana was having an affair with her handsome young co-star. Johnny's possessiveness caused him to show up on the set of the film to keep an eye on his star.

Another motive for Johnny's possessiveness was his desire to engage himself in her business dealings. Hoping to convince her to put him into the role of producer, he reportedly demanded Lana put up $1,000 to option a story called *The Bartered Bride*, with him as producer and her as star. Louella Parsons even printed a column suggesting the film would co-star Frank Sinatra as her leading man. Lana refused to involve Johnny in her business dealings, and he grew frustrated.

One afternoon at the Borehamwood, Hertfordshire studios things got out of hand on the set. During the shoot Johnny Stompanato confronted Sean Connery, accusing him of getting a little too close to his leading lady. Various accounts of the incident have the two men arguing about Connery's intentions toward Lana, but neither star ever admitted to any romance between them. Even so, a jealous Stompanato reportedly pulled a gun on Connery, warning him to stay away from Turner. Connery, the story goes, grabbed the gun in Stompanato's hand and twisted his hand and wrist until he dropped the weapon, causing Johnny to rush off the set in anger. Another story claimed Connery went as far as punching Johnny in the face. Cameras were said to be rolling during the altercation and one story suggests that it was Connery who reported Stompanato to the police, but that was unlikely.

The producers, with support from MGM head Giovanni Di

Lana with Sean Connery during the filming of "Another Time, Another Place."

Stefano, refused to allow Johnny anywhere near the production for the remainder of filming and reported the incident to authorities with the film footage to prove it. Lana was both angered and embarrassed by the incident and felt it was best if Johnny would just leave and let her finish the movie alone. He initially refused, but Scotland Yard was reportedly brought in and Stompanato was deported for breaking England's gun laws. And since Stompanato had entered England using a passport with the name John Steele, they were also able to send him packing for entering the country using a false name.

Lana had invited her daughter to travel to England to keep her company as the holidays approached. "I went over the Christmas holidays expecting him [John] to be there because I knew he had gone there with her. I got there. He wasn't there, I said 'Where's John?'" recalled Cheryl.

"We had some difficulties and I'm no longer seeing him," Lana replied.

However, Lana continued the relationship into the new year as letters she wrote to Johnny in early January would appear in newspapers after the stabbing. While Lana may have wanted distance, part of her continued to be drawn to the man. While records indicated Johnny called Lana once while she was in London and he in the states, Lana called him three times.

Filming wrapped in January 1958 and Lana felt a vacation in a warm sunny place might do her good. She quickly planned a private getaway for herself in Mexico and cabled ahead to make arrangements to stay in her usual villa in Acapulco. Meanwhile, Cheryl headed back to the states for school. "Now, I did not know that they had to call Scotland Yard and have him thrown out of the country. I knew none of that. When it was time for me to go home, to go back to school, my mother was going from London to Mexico for a vacation, the film was finished."

Lana claimed she wanted to keep her arrival in Mexico a

secret, but when she landed at the airport, Stompanato and a group of journalists met her. No studio publicity agent was present, leading her to believe Johnny had somehow managed to set up the press conference. "To this day I can't tell you exactly how John Stompanato knew when I was leaving England or that I was flying to Mexico via Copenhagen," she wrote. "He proved over and over that he had the power to do anything he wanted."

Cheryl also wasn't sure how Johnny ended up with Lana, but recalled that, "Somewhere between London and Mexico, John was waiting for her. I think it was in Stockholm where they changed planes. Anyway, he was in Mexico with her."

Lana's friend and make-up artist Del Armstrong claimed that Lana didn't know Stompanato was on the flight until she was on the plane. Walking to her seat, she spotted him a few seats away. However, it is possible that Lana disclosed her plans to Johnny, but never admitted it to anyone. Since she continued to write to him, and he was probably aware of her frequent Acapulco trips after completing a film, it is possible that Johnny was aware of her plans.

Later in police interviews, Lana would first claim she didn't know how Johnny found her, but when police said they had reason to believe he had been invited, Lana admitted encouraging Stompanato and even paid for it. Police quoted her as saying she had given him thousands of dollars, "not counting the tabs I picked up for him."

While one travel agent remembered Johnny purchasing a ticket to Amsterdam, the second part of his trip to Mexico was believed to have been paid by Lana.

Lana had second thoughts about vacationing with Johnny; though, as she indicated in a letter that she sent to him on January 13, she must have known he knew where she was headed. However, by the time the letter arrived, Stompanato was already on his way to Amsterdam and the letter was forwarded to Acapulco.

Johnny was disappointed to find that his housing in Acapulco put him in a room in the servants quarters, while Lana was located in a private suite. However, Johnny spent much of his time in Lana's room and the two were seen on the beach and boating as well as at several bullfights.

Lana said Johnny continued to be physically abusive during their eight weeks in Mexico, once even pulling a gun on her when she ordered him out of her suite. But even with his bad behavior – or perhaps because of it – Lana found it difficult to let Johnny go. She began to realize she would have to find a way to end things.

Lana's vacation got a boost when she learned that she had been nominated for an Academy Award for her work in *Peyton Place*. She recalled receiving a phone call from her agent, Paul Kohner, who was "bubbling over" with excitement. "Aren't you happy about it?" asked Kohner, who seemed to sense he was more thrilled than his star. "Yes, I guess so … Yes!" Lana replied. She said the news lifted her "out of her gloom and put her on cloud nine."

After nearly two months in Acapulco, Lana and Johnny returned in March 1958, so Lana could prepare for the Academy Awards. When reporters questioned her about her relationship with her traveling companion, Lana admitted she had gone to Acapulco with the former bodyguard of Mickey Cohen from Paris shortly after finishing a motion picture in London. Though, Lana insisted "there is definitely no romantic interest between us."

Cheryl recalled she was in Los Angeles when it was announced her mother had been nominated as Best Actress for *Peyton Place*. Her mother almost immediately planned for her return to Hollywood. "When it was time to come home, my grandmother and I picked them up at the airport - that's the famous picture of all of us."

Cheryl recalled that her mother, grandmother and even Johnny were thrilled with the star's first Oscar nomination. She even said during the trip home there was a lot of talk about the impending awards. "We were all excited about the nomination and on the way home I said to mother, 'Can we go? Can I go?' She said 'Yes, I'm taking you and your grandmother.'"

Reports would claim that pressure from friends was what kept her from taking Johnny to the Oscar awards that year and that this slight "touched off a bitter series of arguments that finally led to the slaying."

Cheryl admitted that she felt things got very tense when Lana shared the news. "I think that was the first time he [Stompanato] had heard that he wasn't going to be her date."

Cheryl would admit that it wasn't until after this that she began to get a better idea of the trouble her mother was in, saying "And she finally sat me down and told me the whole story about having had him thrown out of England when she was filming there because he beat her so badly. How he had threatened her life, my grandmother's life. She couldn't get him out of the house. She couldn't get rid of him."

However, for Cheryl, at the time of the Acapulco vacation, she was still believing her mother was caught up in a whirlwind romance. And she herself had even grown fond of Johnny - so much so, that she wrote him a letter that arrived while he vacationed with her mother in Mexico. Complete with typos and teenage angst, the letter offers no indication of any trouble between Stompanto and her mother.

"Dear Johnny,

First of all please excuse this paper but it's really all I have right now. I just got your letter because I was home for the weekend.

How have you been and how is mother?

Rowena [Cheryl's horse] is just fine. I'm not afraid of her anymore and she acts just the way she use to last summer. I thought for a while I wouldn't be able to handle her but now I know that I can. School is just fine but not getting any easier.

I went to see Johnny Mathis at the Crescendo Sunday night, he was terrific.

Have you been doing any water skiing lately? Please do think of me. I love it.

When are you all coming back? Soon I hope.

Mother and I had a really wonderful time in Europe. I can't remember when we've been that close.

My hair is way past my shoulders now and I have been wearing it in a french roll in back with pixie bangs in front which are all the rage now.

Peter [Cheryl's friend] *and I had a big fight over another guy and he made me so mad by being so jelius* (sic) *that I broke up with him but I really regret it now. Oh well something has to happen.*

I am writing this in study hall as I have finished my work. I thought. I'd better write now before I forgot and put it off. This writing is very messy I know. But the bell is going to ring and I am in a hurry.

Guess what. I'm a member of the student council. Pretty good. Huh!!!

Well the bell just rang so I've got to get now - I'll write again real soon. I promise but now it's your turn.

Love ya and miss ya loads.

- Cherie

P.S. Give my love to mother. Write soon and be good.

Lana, on the other hand, was having misgivings about Johnny and looking for ways to drop the news that not only would he not be escorting her to the Oscar's, but the relationship was coming to an end. Lana's happiness about the nomination gave her new strength. It provided her new resolve for finding a way to put Johnny Stompanato behind her. But that wasn't going to be easy.

NINE

*"Mr. Stompanato grabbed me by
the arms and started shaking me
and cursing me very badly."*
                    - Lana Turner

The Academy Award for Best Performance by an Actress in a Leading Role is one of the most coveted awards presented by the Academy of Motion Picture Arts and Sciences. It recognizes an actress who has delivered an outstanding performance while working within the film industry during that year.

THE ACADEMY AWARDS

A few weeks after Lana returned from Mexico, Cheryl would finally begin to get a true sense of the trouble her mother was in. While she split time between visits with her father and grandmother, the bulk of her time was actually spent at school, leaving little time to spend with Lana alone. And once Johnny entered the picture, he made every effort to monopolize the time with his new

movie star girlfriend and that rarely included a family life with
Lana's teenage daughter.

However, with Johnny so interested in Lana, Cheryl did find
plenty time to get to know the friendly and charming side of Johnny
Stompanato. She found him likeable enough, and even charming
at times. As his relationship with Lana progressed their exchanges
became more difficult, and with Cheryl away at school, and Lana off
filming in London, Cheryl didn't have much of a chance to see the
changes or how they interacted privately. Their interaction in public was always proper, but behind closed doors it was another thing.

Johnny was gone by the time Cheryl
arrived in London to spend Christmas
with her mother. In March, that would all
change.

"I was home from school and
it was the first inkling she had given
me that there were physical problems
between them," recalled Cheryl. "You
know, he was making threats at her. I
said 'Why don't you call Chief Ander-
son?' He was our Chief of Police in Beverly Hills, and a good family
friend. She said 'Oh, I can't, I can't, the publicity, I've got to get him
out of my life, I've got to get rid of him' That's the first time I knew
anything. That's when she told me about Scotland Yard and London
and what happened there and when he had beaten her."

Back from months of filming, Lana didn't really have a place
to call home back in Los Angeles. She rented a bungalow at the Hotel
Bel Air, a boutique hotel in the Bel-Air section of Los Angeles. After
opening in 1946, the 103-room resort on Stone Canyon Road became
a prime escape spot for celebrities, politicians and other dignitaries.
First built by Alphonzo Bell as part of the Bel-Air Estates, it was

primarily used as both office space and riding stables until it was sold off in 1946 and converted into a hotel by Texan entrepreneur Joseph Drown. The hotel's oasis theme featured ficus, fig and palm trees alongside lush gardens of flowers and a swan lake that guests crossed using a footbridge to reach the hotel. Celebrities like Lana enjoyed the privacy the hotel provided as well as the plush amenities and secluded bungalows.

Lana enjoyed having a staff to attend to her needs, but she never intended it to be a long-term living arrangement. To have Cheryl visit and stay with her, she needed something more stable and homey. Now that she was settling back into the Hollywood lifestyle, but without any formal prospects of work, she decided it was a good time to focus on finding a home.

Though the search was a good distraction from her lack of film work, Lana did have a glamorous spotlight shining on her with the news that she was nominated as Best Actress for her work in *Peyton Place*. It was Lana's first and only nomination for the Academy Award and although she would have loved to win, she never really felt she had a chance. Lana never thought the role was one that was really worthy of an Oscar, but because the film was a huge success it was nice to get the recognition. In reality, most of Hollywood had agreed that the award would go hands-down to Joanne Woodward for *The Three Faces of Eve*. Lana's other competition was formidable as well and included Deborah Kerr in *Heaven Knows, Mr. Allison*, Anna Magnani for *Wild is the Wind*, and Elizabeth Taylor for *Raintree County*. Odds really put Lana in fourth or fifth place as the real long shot for taking home the elusive statuette. Even so, the nomination was a win in itself. Considering she was no longer associated with a major studio and had few prospects for work that year, she had managed to come up with a hit when everyone thought her career was over. Lana wasn't the only nominee from the film with both Hope Lange, as rape victim and self-defense murderer Selena Cross, and

Diane Varsi, as Lana's teenager daughter Allison MacKenzie, both were nominated for Best Supporting Actress for the film.

Lana enjoyed the nomination period and claimed she and Johnny even got along for much of it, even though he was displeased about not being able to escort her to the Academy Awards. He may have secretly hoped that he could eventually convince her otherwise if he behaved himself. As Lana shopped for dresses and jewelry for the events surrounding the ceremony Johnny would often escort her. "John asked me to go out to dinner with him, and I surprised him by agreeing. Afterward, we went to a nightclub and danced. As long as John remained in this mood, I could ride it out and eventually get out from under," Lana hoped.

However, Lana claimed that her good spirits were giving Stompanato the wrong impression that the doomed romance had turned around. "He would slip into town and buy me thoughtful gifts, like the lover he had once been," she said. "Later, I learned that I had bought them for myself, as they were charged to my account."

The two would still argue anytime discussion of the Oscars evening came up and Lana tried to avoid bringing it into conversations, for fear it would lead to an eruption from Johnny.

The Academy Awards ceremony was held on March 26, 1958 and was broadcast live on TV from the Pantages Theater. It was the first TV production to be produced by the motion picture industry itself, and the entire show was broadcast from Hollywood. The number of categories was cut down to 24 from 30 in the previous year, though few seemed to notice. The event itself was overshadowed by the death of the previous year's Best Picture producer/winner, Michael Todd. The young husband of Elizabeth Taylor was killed in a plane crash just four days earlier. In addition, Columbia Pictures studio head, Harry Cohn, an original founder of the studio that produced the Best Picture that year, had also died just a month earlier, on February 27, 1958. Hollywood was trying to be tasteful and respectful for the glossy awards evening in light of the recent somber events.

Lana had agreed to take Cheryl and her mother to the Awards instead of Johnny, but he remained close to Lana during much of the period. Lana recalled feeling like "a captive" even while she was excited that her career had been boosted by this wonderful news. She knew, however, that Johnny Stompanato would not provide any help to her reputation or career, if he were seen escorting her to the Academy Awards.

"John assumed he would be escorting me to the Academy Awards ceremony. Not only had I been nominated, but I had also been tapped to present the award for best supporting actor. But I certainly wasn't going to appear among the leading lights of the industry with John on my arm. I screwed up my courage and told him I would not allow him to come. I wanted only my mother and Cheryl there to celebrate with me. Despite his threats and pleadings, I wouldn't budge an inch."

Lana continued to look at real estate rentals in Bel-Air and Beverly Hills, often with Johnny on hand. He wanted to keep tabs on her and in some ways Lana enjoyed the attention and having a man nearby, even if it were Stompanato, but claimed to feel that his attention was demanding. "No matter what I did, he was a hovering presence. It was as though he thought I'd escape somewhere if he freed me for more than an hour," she said.

Still, Lana never planned for him to reside in the house. Johnny remained in his apartment on South Robertson Blvd, near Wilshire Boulevard, in Los Angeles. Not far from La Cienega Park, his place was about 30 minutes from Lana's place at the Bel-Air, and he frequently spent time with her wherever she called home. When she found a suitable home in a neighborhood of stately manors flanked by palm trees on Bedford Drive in Beverly Hills, it was an even closer commute for Johnny with the house being less than 10 minutes away by car. The house was Moorish in design and included a tennis court out back. Lana felt that it was perfect for her and Cheryl. She particularly liked the glamorous pink bedroom, complete with plush pink carpeting. She rented the house fully furnished and set the move-in date for April 1. "I came home only a week or two later, and it was Easter holiday," Cheryl recalled. "She had rented a home on Bedford in the meantime, so I was moving back in with her."

With Lana still residing at the Bel-Air-Hotel, Johnny stood close by on Oscar night as she prepared for the ceremony. In addition to Johnny, her dressmaker and hairdresser helped prepare her for what would be her only chance at winning an Oscar.

Still annoyed that he wouldn't be attending the awards with her, he demanded details on when she expected to be through with her event. "But you're not going to the ball afterward?" he asked.

"If I win, which is unlikely, I have to go," she responded.

The two tried to keep the arguing to a minimum in front of her dressing attendants that evening, but Stompanato continued to push her for specifics about her evening. Before things heated up the limousine pulled up with Cheryl and Lana's mother Mildred inside, all gussied up for their first Academy Awards ceremony.

Cheryl told Lana she'd never looked more beautiful, and Lana was thrilled to see Cheryl "ecstatic" about attending the Oscars. Lana's dress was a strapless gown made of white lace. It was form fitting through her torso and down to her knees. From there it flared out with three more layers of lace stiffed by tulle. Lana said the dress "evoked the image of a mermaid."

Against the tan of her skin from her recent Acapulco trip, she radiated from behind the white lace. She had her hair cut short and bleached to an almost platinum white. She finished the look with earrings, necklace and bracelet of shimmering diamonds. "I really wanted to knock them out of their seats as I walked down the ramp of the Pantages Theatre," Lana recalled.

"Well, Lana my dear, win or lose tonight, you can really be proud of yourself," said Lana's mother. "Maybe you'll win."

Cheryl wanted the evening to be special for her as well. Requesting to be referred to as "Cherie," because she hated "Cheryl," she saw the evening as her formal debut as an adult woman. Lana tried to make it special, having a dress designed specifically for her that evening. It was in her favorite color of green, and Lana had it made of chiffon. While Cheryl wanted strapless, Lana preferred she wore sleeves, but the two compromised and had the dress made with a halter and a built in bra. The outfit was completed with a white ermine stole around her shoulders.

The scene at the Oscars, while certainly glamorous, had a more local feel back then, as Lana remembered it. As her car pulled up to the corner of Hollywood and Vine, she still felt that the night was magical. "In the fifties it just looked like any other corner in any downtown in America, with a department store, a drugstore, and a restaurant. Next to the luggage shop, the marquee of the Pantages, its thin spire with fanciful lettering, glowed brightly in the neon of the street."

Lana exited the car dressed to the nines, but wearing what she called were "dainty, high-heeled slippers." As she hurried down the red carpet entrance past fans shouting "Lana, Lana!" from the bleachers, she lost one of her shoes in the crowd outside. Still, she managed to get inside and limped down the aisle trying to hide the missing shoe, until she reached her seat. Her publicist then headed back outside to try and locate the missing shoe, since Lana was due to present onstage and couldn't very well walk across the theater – and national television – with only one shoe.

With the shoe recovered and everyone seated the ceremony

began and shortly thereafter, an usher came to escort Lana backstage to present the award for Best Supporting Actor. It was in fact a change to tradition when the producers put one of the four major acting awards so early in the show. Shortly after the first opening number with Mae West, 12 minutes in, Lana was getting ready for her live television debut.

Lana with Oscar winner Red Buttons at the Academy Awards.

Once backstage, she was greeted by a collection of familiar faces and she was "thoroughly delighted" as she waited for her cue to head to the podium. Even though she was a huge star and had been in the spotlight for years, this evening was special. For not only was it her only time as a Best Actress nominee, but it was also her first appearance on live television.

With hosts including Bob Hope, Rosalind Russell, Jack Lemmon and Jimmy Stewart, it was Stewart who introduced Lana to give out the first acting statuette.

She said that when it was time to go on she said it was a thrill as Jimmy Stewart announced her, and she walked onstage. "The audience responded with gasps followed by a torrent of applause for the blonde, tanned vision I had created as I walked onstage. I felt I was floating on a sea of warmth and love," she wrote in her autobiography.

"Thank you so much," she said to Stewart, who was about to exit the stage. "Oh, but Jimmy, don't leave, please," she cooed.

"Why?" he asked. "Ya nervous?"

"No …," she responded. "It's just that … I like you."

"Well," he muttered and gulping. "Now I'm nervous."

The audience laughed and Lana felt more at ease, launching into the purpose of her appearance, to announce the nominees and winner of Best Supporting Actor.

She read the names of the nominees, secretly hoping her friend Red Buttons would win, even though two of her co-stars from *Peyton Place* were in the running. When she opened the envelope and announced "Red Buttons for *Sayonara*," she was as happy as the audience. "He ran up the ramp, and we hugged each other," she recalled. "When I handed him the statuette, he kissed me impetuously as the audience roared."

Later, as John Wayne announced the nominees for the Best Actress award, Lana saw herself in *Peyton Place* as shots of the actors displayed on the stage screen. She was honored and amazed to have made it this far. Aside from Joanne Woodward, Lana was the only other Best Actress nominee in attendance, so all eyes were on the two women. She was sure she wouldn't win and claimed she felt quite calm as the nominees were announced. "Before they even announced it, I knew Joanne Woodward had won, and God knows she deserved the honor for her multiple roles in *The Three Faces of Eve*."

Lana remained in her seat, smiling as Woodward rushed onto stage and gushed her quick thank yous for the award. The ceremony rolled on, and Lana's moments were behind her.

Once the awards were over Lana, her mother and Cheryl left the theater to head to the Beverly Hilton to attend the celebratory ball. However, their driver had fallen asleep in their limo and missed the pick-up time. When the car failed to appear the three jumped into a taxi for the quick trip to the after party. Even though Lana had lost the award, she was excited to still be celebrating the nomination. It would mark the only occasion where she would be up for the elusive statuette, and she intended to make the most of it.

Lana very much wanted to share the evening with her daughter, but was also conscious of the press. "At the party tonight, as the photographers come around to the table, I don't want to see a cigarette in your hand," she made her daughter promise. "No drinks either. I don't want to see pictures come out with glasses on the table."

"Yes, Mother," Cheryl assured her.

"You make sure there's nothing in front of you. I don't care if it's ginger ale. You're fourteen years old and you know how that would look."

Lana was sure she'd never be voted mother of the year with her sex symbol image, but she was careful not to make matters worse with the media getting the idea that she was a bad or absent mother.

TEN

"As he let go of me, he said, 'That's just to let you know I am not kidding. Don't think you can ever get away.'"

- Lana Turner

*After losing the Academy Award for Best Actress, Lana would
suffer a more severe blow when Johnny paid her back for not
escorting her to the ceremony.*

THE ATTACK

"That night all my tensions just seemed to float away on the
wave of sound," Lana recalled as both she and Cheryl were invited to
dance at the post-Oscar bash. She felt the evening away from Johnny
and surrounded by the glittering Hollywood crowd was "just the
tonic" she needed.

She danced the night away and forgot about her troubles at
home, focusing on catching up with old friends like Clark Gable,
Cary Grant, Sean Connery and others. Joanne Woodward even came
by with her husband, Paul Newman, and Lana had the chance to

congratulate her on her well-deserved win. As the party ended, the trio headed home in their limo, dropping her mother off first and then returning to the Bel-Air Hotel with Cheryl, as Lana had invited her to stay the night with her since it would be late.

Cheryl remembered, "When we got back to the hotel, I spent the night with her after the awards, he was there."

Lana claimed Johnny went into a rage after having watched Lana on television at the Academy Awards. His anger at not being invited to share the evening with her or having his own moment in the spotlight as the lover of an Academy Award nominated actress led him to take out his frustrations on her.

Lana didn't realize Johnny was there. She and Cheryl only noted that music was playing in the suite when they entered, and it wasn't until she went into her bedroom and turned on the light that she saw Johnny there waiting for her in the dark in the chaise lounge near her bed. "You'll never leave me home again!" he shouted. "That's the last time."

Lana, Johnny and Cheryl at the airport after her trip back from Acapulco. All appeared happy to be together.

He reportedly berated Lana for not winning and then shamed her for her increased reliance on alcohol and partying without him, accusing her of being drunk and for having too good a time without him. Things escalated when he began slapping her face.

"He cracked me a second time, this time knocking me down," Lana recalled. "I staggered back against the chaise and slid to the floor. He yanked me up and began hitting me with his fists. I went flying across the room into the bar, sending glasses shattering on the floor."

Picking her up again, he grabbed her shoulders and peered down at her.

"Now do you understand?" he asked. "You will never leave me out of something like that again ... Ever," Johnny threatened.

In the early morning hours of the day after the Academy Awards ceremony, when she should have been sleeping with dreams of her night in the spotlight, Lana lay bruised and bleeding in bed. "Underlying everything was my shame," said Lana. "I was so ashamed. I didn't want anybody to know my predicament, how foolish I'd been, how I'd taken him at face value and been completely duped."

"I overheard them having a horrible fight," Cheryl said later. "I didn't see it, but he did beat her up, because she had a black eye the next morning. I left to go back to school and I said, 'Please mother, you've got to get somebody to get rid of him, get him out of your life. Please call the police?'"

Lana asked Cheryl to promise not to tell anyone, including her grandmother or father for fear it might make matters worse. While Cheryl never saw Johnny hit Lana that night, she did see the injuries after her visit in London over Christmas, and now after the Academy Awards. "[There were] awful fights, screaming and yelling and smashing glasses and just, you know, things I wasn't used to hearing," Cheryl recalled. "And she finally sat me down and told me the whole story about having had him thrown out of England when she was filming there, because he beat her so badly. How he had threatened her life, my grandmother's life. She couldn't get him out of the house. She couldn't get rid of him. Again, her reaction was, 'Well, mother, call the police.'"

However, Lana refused to call the police. She not only feared how Stompanato or his fellow gangster friends might react – toward her, or her mother and daughter – but also she feared how the press and her fans would see it. "That was last thing in the world she would do because of the publicity," Cheryl said. "You know, I mean, it would have been, she felt, the end of her career."

According to Beverly Hills Police Chief Anderson, Lana's mother called him one week before the slaying on Good Friday to say her daughter was frightened of Stompanato, and she needed advice on what to do. Anderson told Mildred Turner the police could only get involved if Lana herself would come in and report the threats. Lana never did.

ELEVEN

*"I truthfully thought she had
hit him in the stomach ... I still
never saw a blade."*

- Lana Turner

Lana had no idea what had actually happened. In fact, for a moment Johnny had no idea either. The nine-inch butcher knife Cheryl held in her hand thrust forward with Johnny walking right into it. "For three ghastly heartbeats our bodies fused," remembered Cheryl.

THE FATAL STABBING

The knife hadn't even been in the house a week. Johnny, in fact, had been with Lana when she picked up the set of cutlery on March 31 in a Beverly Hills hardware store. As Lana recalled it, he even selected the knife that would end his life; and at the time of the killing, she recalled it still had the price tag on it.

It was one of the few housewares Lana and Johnny brought

into the rented home. MGM hairstylist Sydney Guilaroff, remembered seeing Lana in the store buying the knife that day while also shopping at the store.

While the house she rented was fully furnished, shortly before moving in Lana realized, after a pre-move inspection of the house, that it was missing a few things. So, with Johnny's help, she found a store to pick up some inexpensive silverware, a set of china, pots and pans, kitchen knives and a set of carving knives.

In business since 1926, Pioneer Hardware was a local shop with a selection of fine housewares any celebrity might need. Lana remembered Johnny had driven with her to the store that morning with Johnny picking out the knife that would ultimately kill him. "I didn't bother to look at the carving set John selected," she recalled. "After all, knives were knives to me … he was the expert in that department."

Lana arranged to have her purchases delivered to the house

Johnny's car parked outside 730 N. Bedford the night of his death.

on April 1, her and Cheryl's formal move-in date. Though the purchases would help stock the kitchen with required items, Lana was never much of a cook and selected the house for a host of other reasons. The quiet neighborhood with a lawn and backyard would provide a warm family setting that Lana wanted her image to project, even if it was always more an aspiration than reality. Even the tennis courts would offer the lure of activity and social interaction, but wouldn't be a place Lana would find herself frequenting even if she had stayed longer.

The hectic move-in was made less hectic for the simple fact that the house was nearly fully furnished; so, aside from clothes and personal belongings, most of the heavy lifting was already done. Johnny stood close by nonetheless.

On April 2, Lana awoke to news that her friend and former co-star, Judy Garland, faced arrest after a warrant was issued on tax evasion charges. She was required to appear before court in New York Friday morning, April 4. Reports noted that Judy had to use her concert gowns and jewelry as collateral in order to make a $10,000 bond to gain her release. Lana was thankful such an embarrassing event wasn't facing her. By Saturday morning, April 5, Judy's problems would seem small compared to the firestorm about to be unleashed in Lana's life.

The six-bedroom, six-bath house she moved into was originally built in 1930 for *Gone with the Wind* actress Laura Hope Crews. Crews played Aunt Pittypat in the film, but had been working in silent films back as early as 1915 and had roles in a collection of sound features between 1929 and 1942. She used her success to build her dream home. Crews died in 1942 and the house was sold, eventually turning into a rental property.

At 6,769 square feet, the home was really more than Lana needed, but what sold Lana was the lavish pink master bedroom on the second floor. The bedroom featured a double bed with pink satin bed coverings and a matching chair and ottoman in the corner beside a fireplace. Directly in front of the bed was a massive wardrobe to house Lana's large collection of clothes and jewelry. Bedside tables with lamps and other knickknacks, some of which would be Lana's own, made the room feel homey. A spacious bathroom to the right of the wardrobe center provided privacy from the rest of the house. Directly outside the bedroom door was a stairway leading downstairs and quick access to the kitchen.

Cheryl's room was also on the second floor, down the hall from Lana's. The second floor was accessed by a center staircase and consisted of only the two large bedroom suites connected by a passageway leading to an entrance hall with French doors that opened onto a large balcony overlooking the street and driveway.

Cheryl recalled loving the house the moment she saw it. Driving up the curved driveway, the white colonial was offset by dark black shutters. Cheryl recalled Johnny being the one to first bring her to the new home.

Lana's rented home at 730 North Bedford Drive was on a quiet street in the heart of Beverly Hills. The house came fully furnished and Lana loved the pink bedroom, but her stay would be quite brief as she would not return after the killing.

April 4, 1958 was Good Friday. With Easter Sunday fast approaching, Tinsel Town was in the mood to put on a show. A parade through Hollywood from the Beverly Hilton to the Beverly Hills Hotel snarled downtown traffic as a collection of local celebrities from movies and television rode on the back seats and hoods of convertibles. Fans waved and cheered from the sidewalks. It was the first year the event would be held. Singer Erin O'Brien and her horse Rusty, adorned in Easter bonnets, joined other stars with the parade through town at 1 pm., followed by a luncheon in the ballroom at the hotel to raise funds for the Easter Seals. It was one of many events that filled up the day. Passover also began and religious events were scheduled across the city. The Los Angeles Metropolitan Transit Authority also used the day to switch routes for three of its downtown bus lines, adding to the confusion on the roadways.

While the smog was at a minimum, the day was partly cloudy with scattered showers, and they were expected to continue through Saturday. It wasn't expected to warm up much either, with a high of only 65. The low that night would hit 53. The damp day gave people an extra push to head indoors, with local churches celebrating Good Friday, masses went from noon to 3 p.m. If you weren't the church-going type, the movie theater was be a good escape. *Run Silent, Run Deep* with Burt Lancaster and Lana's former co-star, Clark Gable, was playing, as was Bob Hope in *Paris Holiday*. Both films would get some competition with Danny Kaye's *Merry Andrew* premiering on Good Friday.

For Cheryl, movies and church were not on her mind. She was busy getting settled into her new bedroom that morning and spent the better part of the afternoon with her father. Returning to her new home around 5:30 pm, she recalled, "I'd been living at my grandmother's. It was Good Friday and I'd come back from having lunch with my dad."

Lana and Johnny returned home before Cheryl, arriving about

4:30 after having met there around 2 pm when he arrived to pick her up. After arriving, Lana said, "We put some things in the – in my station wagon to take back to the store and we drove into Beverly Hills."

Since Lana was still getting settled, she had been busy arranging her personal belongings and buying small odds and ends for the kitchen, bathrooms, her bedroom and Cheryl's room to go along with the furnishings the house had already. She explained she and Johnny headed down Beverly Drive, "to the first store and returned some purchases I had made Thursday and purchases of a few other things to replace them. Then we walked up the street to the second store to buy some – buy more light bulbs and then I went across the street to the pet shop."

Lana said the two were out shopping longer than she planned and that she needed to get home. "I had told my two friends that I would be home about 3:30. So, when I walked in, they teasingly said that I was late, so that is the way I know it was almost 4:30."

With Johnny by her side, Lana sat down and "chatted for a while and my daughter came home around 5:30."

Cheryl greeted her mother and her friends and the group again spoke a few minutes, and then Cheryl went upstairs. Lana's guests invited her to dinner and that's when the evening took a fateful turn. "My friends asked me if I would be able to perhaps have dinner with them and I said 'No, I don't think so," because it was very late notice and my maid does not live in, and if I was going to go out, I would have to arrange with my mother so that she would either come over to the house or my daughter would go to her house, because she had never been left alone."

Lana said Johnny that became annoyed, explaining he "was upset that I had even considered the idea of having dinner with friends, but I had not seen them for a long time and he said, 'You mean I cannot come along?' And I said, 'Well, surely I have a right to be able to see some people without your always being there and there is nothing wrong just to be able to sit and discuss our friendship. It was friendships that were long ago that you didn't even know about."

Lana tried to diffuse the situation by saying, "Anyway, I am not going to have dinner with them tonight, perhaps I will be able to Saturday night. I will have to call my mother and see if she is busy. If she is not, perhaps she can spend the evening here with the child or take her to dinner."

Lana said Johnny left "at a quarter to 6, saying that he would telephone me back at 7 or 7:30."

"My friends left at about a quarter of 7," Lana remembered, adding that Johnny did, in fact, call her back, "possibly about 10 minutes to 8 and he said that he would be over in a little while and it was sometime after 8 o'clock when he arrived."

During the time when Johnny was gone, one of her friends made a comment about Stompanato's age, suggesting he was younger than Lana realized. She's claimed that Johnny had told her that he was in his 40s, but the friend told her that he had to be in his early 30s, because he had attended school with an acquaintance that was about the same age. Lana became angry that Johnny had lied to her time and time again about his age and confronted him about it when he returned that evening. The two argued about his lies and also about Lana's refusal to give him $3,600 to cover a gambling debt.

Upstairs, Cheryl had changed out of her clothes. Wearing a robe with a slip and brassiere underneath, she settled down into her room, turned on the television and began to work on a school term paper. "I was doing homework, a paper, and they [Lana and Johnny] started having a big argument."

Cheryl recalled that the argument started innocently enough, but soon grew more frightening. "Mother found out he was 10 years younger than he said he was."

Lana said the argument started downstairs, but that the two

"went back upstairs to my bedroom, both of us talking at once, he more violently. All I said was, 'There's no use discussing it any further; and I want you to leave me alone.' He grabbed me by the arms … and started shaking me and cursing me very badly, and saying that, as he had told me before, no matter what I did, how I tried to get away, he would never leave me – that if he said jump, I would jump, if he said hop, I would hop – and I would have to do anything and everything he told me or he'd cut my face or cripple me."

As *The Phil Silvers Show* played on the TV, Cheryl recalled Lana coming into her room to tell her she and Johnny were done, and he was leaving. Johnny followed her into Cheryl's room and refused to leave. He grew angrier and began to make threats. As the argument grew more intense, Cheryl became concerned Johnny might actually do something. While Lana and Johnny were still arguing in the open, Cheryl began to think about protection and left her room, heading downstairs. "I ran down to the living room area and the kitchen, looking for something, anything. If I had found a baseball bat I would have taken that, but I found a knife sitting on the counter. I grabbed that and I ran back up the stairs."

By the time Cheryl got back upstairs Lana and Johnny were still arguing, this time in Lana's bedroom, but the door was open. Lana said Johnny had grabbed her by the arms, but she had pulled away. "I broke away from his holding me – holding me, and I turned around, and my daughter was standing there, and I said, 'Please, Cheryl, please don't listen to any of this. Please go back to your own room.'"

Lana recalled, "She looked at me, and I think that – as if to say, 'Are you sure, Mother?' Because I know I repeated it, and I begged her, I said, 'Please, Cheryl, don't listen to this. I beg you to go back to your room.'"

Lana didn't recall Cheryl holding a knife at the time. Cheryl, on the other hand, recalled having the knife before Lana closed the door, so she brought the knife into her own bedroom and hoped the drama might end, but kept the knife, "in case he tried to hurt Mother," she later told police.

Cheryl found it virtually impossible to ignore the yelling coming from Lana's bedroom across the hallway. "He was in there with her. So, being a nosey kid I guess, I tiptoed down the hall to listen to what was going on and got very, very frightened by the threats

Johnny Stompanato

he was making against her, and my grandmother and me. I mean, death threats that we would be cut into little pieces. We didn't see that kind of stuff on TV then so this was very frightening."

Outside the bedroom, Cheryl called to her mother and Johnny, trying to stop the fighting. "I was, you know, hoping to get them apart," Cheryl recalled.

"Cheryl, get away from that door!" Lana demanded. "I'm not going to tell you again!"

But Cheryl wouldn't leave. She recalled continuing to plead with her mother to stop arguing and open the door. "And she wouldn't open the door," Cheryl said. "She said, 'Go back to your room. John is leaving.' And, of course, he didn't leave. And then I started hearing the threats that he was making that he was going to cut her face, that he was going to kill my grandmother. 'And I'll get your daughter, too.' "

She heard Johnny say something like, "You'll never get away from me. I'll cut you good, baby. No one will ever look at that pretty face again." And as the threats escalated, Cheryl grew even more fearful for her mother's safety. Having not been present for most of their evenings together, or sharing the home with Lana when Johnny was in the picture, this was a new experience, and she wasn't sure what she should do.

Cheryl recalled the conversation with her mother after the Oscars and how she had confided in her that Johnny had made previous threats to hurt her. She also had not been present for a lot of the private interaction between the pair and was not prepared for the volatility that began unraveling around her. "I could not hear exactly what they were saying. Mother told me he threatened her and would kill her if she tried to leave him and she was afraid to call and get some protection. She was very afraid and she just told me about all the times he had threatened her. He said he would sit back and watch all that happened and he was laughing."

Eventually, things quieted down. With the door to Lana's bedroom still closed, Johnny began collecting his things and preparing to leave. He went to the closet and gathered up a set of his clothes which where hanging on several heavy, wooden hangers. Meanwhile,

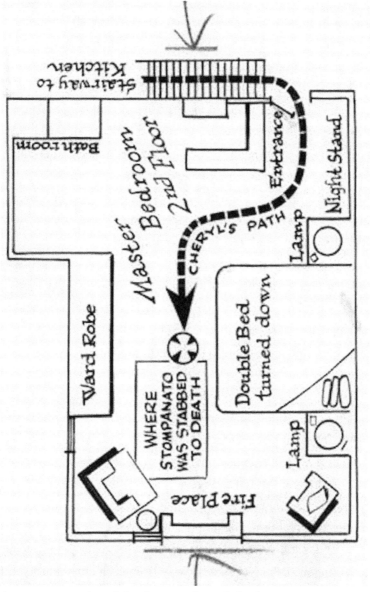

A courtroom sketch laying out Lana's bedroom

outside the bedroom, Cheryl grew concerned when things got quiet, imagining what Johnny might have done to her mother. Armed with the knife, Cheryl begged her mother to open the door once again. This time Lana did. "I am not sure how long Cheryl was outside the door. I know that when I opened it, at one point, she was there."

Johnny was still angry as Lana opened the door for him to leave. Standing between Cheryl and Johnny, Lana had opened the door to allow Johnny to exit. He was facing the door and looking at Lana. He had his arm raised up with his hand over his shoulder holding the clothes he was carrying. To Cheryl, looking past Lana, she saw the gesture in a threatening way. To Cheryl, all she could see was his arm and in his hand she thought he was holding some sort of weapon. "She just came inside the door, and the door was open," Lana recalled. "He was standing there with a jacket and shirt over his shoulders and he kept on and on and on with these threats. And Cheryl said, 'John, don't talk to mother like that.'"

With Lana positioned between Johnny and Cheryl, neither had a clear view of the other, or what they were holding. As Johnny moved toward Lana and the open doorway, his upraised arm held something Cheryl saw as a threat. As she came into the bedroom, passing Lana and into Johnny's path she thrust out her arm, holding the sharp knife in her hand. Lana's failed to notice the knife and said from her vantage point it looked like "Cheryl had punched Johnny in the stomach." Stompanato stepped back, sucked in his breath and jerked as if he had just been hit and uttered his last words, "Oh, my God, Cheryl, what have you done?"

To Lana it seemed strange at first, "… they came together. They parted. He grabbed his stomach, and he walked a little way, made almost a half turn, and dropped on his back."

While at first it appeared as if Cheryl was just poking Johnny with her finger, as the two backed away from each other and Johnny landed on the floor, Lana realized something serious had happened.

Cheryl still held the knife in her hand, but when she realized what she had done she dropped the knife as Johnny stumbled back, gasped, and fell to the floor. A few drops of blood landed on the carpet.

Cheryl recalled the incident years later, saying, "I was so terrified and I was trying to find something to protect us from him. Anyway, I was outside her door again. The door flew open; there was a little hallway there, and he was coming toward me, but looking back yelling at her, she was behind him. He had his arm raised, his right arm, up over his head. Now from my view, it looked like he was about to hit her. What he was actually doing was carrying some clothes on the hangers; you know how you do behind your back. And he turned and saw me, and I was right there, and literally we walked into each other, and he walked into the knife. It was over very quickly."

Cheryl recalled Johnny looking at her just after the stabbing, saying, 'My God, Cheryl, what have you done?' before stumbling back and falling to the floor beside the pink armchair in Lana's bedroom and inches from the bed Lana and Johnny had shared. He was dead within moments."

With his eyes closed and wheezing awfully, Johnny lay dying on the pink carpet of Lana Turner's bedroom. It was approximately 9:20 p.m. Cheryl backed away and dropped the knife. "I turned and ran back to my bedroom and called my father, who called the police. From then on it was a huge blur of activity and police, cameras and all that stuff," recalled Cheryl.

Lana quickly realized something serious had happened and ran to Johnny. She could hear him choking and gurgling, but saw no wound. She knelt down and pulled up his sweater and saw a small slice in his abdomen, but very little blood.

TWELVE

"Mr. Stompanato was making very dreadful sounds in his throat of gasping ... terrible sounds."

- Lana Turner

While the scent of Lana's favorite perfume Tuberose by Mary Chess, flowed softly through the bedroom, the scene was anything but romantic and light. The darkness and dampness of the outside had taken over the inside as well. The scene for Lana seemed surreal.

AFTER THE KILLING

"I still did not see there was blood or a wound," Lana recalled in the immediate moments after the stabbing. "I remember only barely hearing my daughter sobbing and I ran into my bathroom … and I grabbed a towel. I didn't know what to do."

Cheryl left the room in tears, and Lana picked the knife up off the floor where Cheryl had dropped it and put it into the sink in the pink marble bar in her bedroom. She immediately thought to call her doctor for help. "I couldn't remember my doctor's number, so I called my mother and asked her to call my doctor." It was the only phone number that came to her.

"Are you sick?", her mother asked after she demanded she get the doctor to the house.

A policeman inspects Johnny's wound before his body is removed from the home and transported to the morgue.

"Don't ask me, Mother."

"Lana, you sound dreadful. Is Cheryl alright? Tell me what's the matter."

Lana claimed she looked at Johnny's motionless body on the floor and uttered, "Mother, John is dead."

With Lana in such a state, Mildred hung up and called the doctor immediately to have him meet her at the house. "I told Dr. McDonald to go to 730 – I thought I had said Bedford, but I had said Beverly," Mildred later recalled.

"I rushed, I got my coat, and I really rushed. In fact, I was going fast, and when I turned in, [to 730 Bedford] I thought, 'Did I give the doctor the right address?'"

Lana tried calling her mother back, but she was already on the way to the house.

Johnny was clearly having trouble breathing, and in an attempt to save him Lana began giving Johnny mouth-to-mouth resuscitation. "I called to Cheryl, 'Cheryl, Cheryl,' and she came running in and I said, 'Help me. I don't know what to do with – maybe some cold cloths.' So, she went into my bathroom. She came back with two wet wash cloths."

Lana said she put one of the cold cloths on Johnny's forehead while Cheryl kept repeating, "Mamma, I didn't mean to do it, I didn't mean to do it."

After rushing back to her room, Cheryl's first instinct was to pick up the phone and call her father. She knew he was working, and the restaurant's phone number was clear enough to quickly dial the numbers from the phone in her new bedroom.

Stephen Crane was the host and owner of the Luau, a Polynesian-themed restaurant on Rodeo Drive in Beverly Hills. Opened in 1953, it was quickly becoming a celebrity hotspot because of its uncommon Hawaiian and Polynesian inspired Tiki decor and its high profile customers. In the years after its popularity began to grow,

Crane became well known in the restaurant industry for his innovative tableware and dinnerware and anything relating to the trending Polynesian-themed restaurant.

Crane had started off his career in Hollywood as an actor, but the career never took off, and the food industry beckoned him. It was a wise decision and, by 1958, things were going so well that he was in the process of expanding his company, Stephen Crane Associates.

Crane had recently signed a deal with Sheraton hotels across the U.S. and Canada, opening a Polynesian-themed chain of restaurants called Kon Tiki. The restaurants would be opening over the next few years in Sheraton Hotels in Montreal, Portland, Chicago, Cincinnati, Cleveland, Honolulu, and Boston. He also had several other restaurants in Dallas and Toronto called Ports o' Call. While the expanding business took a lot of his energy, his flagship location in Beverly Hills was what put him on the map, and every evening

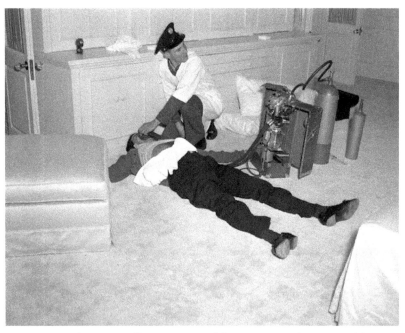

Doctors and paramedics were unable to save Johnny, and he died in the bedroom shortly after the stabbing.

when the place was open, Cheryl knew he would be there to welcome his dining guests.

Crane knew it was a bit past 9 pm, because the dinner rush was ending and he had just sat down to eat something when one of his staff motioned to him that he was wanted on the telephone. Picking up the receiver to say "hello," he heard Cheryl cry out, "Daddy, Daddy, come quick. Something terrible has happened."

"What's the matter?" He asked his daughter.

"Don't ask any questions, Daddy, just hurry."

Crane hung up the phone and quickly headed to the door, but just as he exited, he realized he didn't actually have his car with him because he had been dropped off earlier. He turned around in the doorway and glanced back inside. At the bar, he saw a friend he recognized, Phil Terini, and asked him, "Will you please do me a favor and drive me someplace?"

Terini said, "Sure."

"We got into his car," Crane recalled. "I told him I wanted to go up to Miss Turner's house for a minute. I couldn't remember – then I remembered it was Bedford, 730 Bedford. I had never been there before. We looked at the first block and it was 600 and then we went up to the next block. I was looking out the window and I saw a light in the doorway."

Terini stopped the car and Crane got out. Just then, he heard Cheryl call "Daddy," He responded he was coming. "As I ran up the driveway, Cherie turned and ran. I said, 'Wait a minute, baby.' And I caught up with her as she went up the stairs. Cheryl turned and went to the right, into the [Lana's] bedroom. And when I entered I saw Lana and she came up to me and said, 'Something terrible had happened.' I then looked over her shoulder and I saw Mr. Stompanato on his back on the floor."

"What happened, Cherie?" asked her father.

"I did it, Daddy, but I didn't mean to. He was going to hurt

Mommie," his daughter told him.

Lana recalled her ex-husband saying, "Oh, my God. This is terrible."

To which she responded, "Yes, I know it's horrible. And I don't know what to do except what I have done. And the doctor should be here any minute. We told him it was an emergency."

Cheryl began to sob, crying, "I didn't mean to ... I didn't mean to."

Lana put her arm around her and responded, "I know you didn't."

"I just wanted to protect you."

Cheryl's shock was beginning to get the better of her, and her father feared she might faint. He walked up to her and put his arm around her. He then took her back to her bedroom, across the hall, and tried to calm her down.

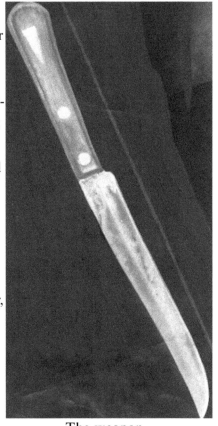

The weapon

"Daddy, will it be all right? Tell me it will be all right," Cheryl sobbed.

"Yes, I am sure it will be," he told her.

Lana's mother arrived shortly before the doctor, rushing up the stairs and into Lana's room. "And as I went in, somewhere I saw Stephen [Crane]. I don't know whether it was – I really don't know where."

Mildred then saw Lana. "But Lana seemed to meet me, and

she – she said, 'Oh, Mother, it's dreadful, horrible,' or something."

Mildred then asked where Cheryl was. "They said she was in her bedroom. I had only been there a second, just a few moments, when the phone rang. I honestly don't know if I answered it or whether somebody else answered it, and said, 'It is Dr. McDonald,' and I took it. I said 'Doctor, did I give you 730 North Bedford? Where are you?"

Doctor McDonald replied, "I am out at Beverly, but I am only two minutes away. I will be right there."

Mildred hung up the phone and went to her granddaughter. Cheryl looked up at her grandmother, asking, "He is going to be alright, isn't he, Granny."

Mildred Turner responded to her granddaughter, "Yes, everything is going to be alright."

But Stephen Crane looked at Lana, thinking, "I was pretty sure it wasn't alright."

Stephen Crane recalled arriving before the doctor, because he remembered hearing someone – he believed Lana – say, "Hurry up, Doctor. Right this way. Hurry up please."

Within minutes the doctor arrived at the house and rushed upstairs. Doctor McDonald gave Johnny a shot of adrenaline, directly into his heart, in hopes of keep his heart beating until paramedics arrived, but it was too late. Johnny Stompanato was already dead. Another doctor was also called to the scene and confirmed the diagnosis.

Moments later, someone came to the door, most likely the doctor, and asked Stephen Crane if he could help move the cars, including Stompanato's 1957 Ford Thunderbird, that were blocking the driveway, as the ambulance was coming. "I told Cheryl, 'Daddy will be back,' and I went downstairs. And there were some cars parked in the driveway and there weren't any keys in them, so we pushed them. There's an incline down the driveway, and we pushed the cars down into the street."

"Lana, I can't get a heartbeat," Dr. McDonald said, and Lana knew Johnny was dead. Doctor McDonald was the one who supposedly gave Lana the best piece of advice when he suggested she call Jerry Giesler. They were going to need a lawyer.

The English-styled estate of Jerry Giesler was built on a triangle of land between Camden and Benedict Canyon Drives and Sunset Boulevard. Located at 901 Benedict Canyon Drive in Beverly Hills, the house was built in 1948. Surrounded by an acre of im-

Johnny, dead on the floor of Lana Turner's bedroom

maculately landscaped grounds, it was only about five minutes away from Lana Turner's newly rented home on North Bedford Drive. Giesler was at home the evening of Good Friday when his phone rang at about 9:30 pm.

"This is Lana Turner," the voice on the other end of the line said. "Something terrible has happened. Could you please come to my house?", said the distraught voice.

Giesler was a prominent Los Angeles lawyer who first found his way into the media spotlight when he served as an apprentice to Earl Rogers in the defense of the nation's top criminal defense attorney, Clarence Darrow. During the trial, Darrow and Rogers were impressed with Jerry's knowledge of the law, but Jerry remained mostly out of the limelight with Darrow arguing the case. Giesler was admitted to the bar in 1910 and would spend decades artfully defending the accused. His skills became so valuable in Hollywood that a common catchphrase – "Get me Giesler" was known around town, when someone needed help getting out of a sticky legal situation.

For Lana, the evening had become more than just sticky – she was stuck – between a rock and a hard place – with a dead lover lying on her bedroom floor. Upon realizing Stompanato was dead, Dr. McDonald looked up from Johnny's side to Lana, who stood by helplessly, and suggested she call Jerry Giesler for legal advice. She took his advice.

While Lana waited for her lawyer and the police, she found Cheryl sitting in her bedroom, "trembling violently."

"Sitting close by her, rocking her back and forth, trying to quiet her shaking." Lana didn't speak to her about the events, only saying, "Shhh, darling. Don't cry. Don't cry."

Before Jerry Giesler headed to Lana's home, he made a quick call to Detective Fred Otash and asked him to meet him at his new star client's home, feeling he might need an extra pair of hands.

Otash was a former Hollywood police officer, who now

made his living as a private investigator. He worked frequently for Hollywood Research Incorporated, a business that made its living by digging up dirt and providing juicy details for the tabloid magazine *Confidential*. Giesler also knew it would be better to have Otash working for him rather than digging up dirt for the tabloid.

Some reports suggest that Otash was already aware of the Turner-Stompanato affair after having been hired briefly by Cheryl's father, Stephen Crane, to keep an eye on his daughter, though it seems unlikely. Rumors circulated suggesting that Crane may have been afraid of Stompanato's involvement with his daughter, as well as with his ex-wife.

Fred Otash claimed he was on the scene before the police and ambulance arrived, going as far as saying that he was the one who removed the knife from the dead man's body, though it's unlikely he was telling the truth. He once claimed he was the one who placed the murder weapon in Cheryl's hand, so fingerprints would support claims that she was the killer, though many felt his story was more to promote himself and sell his own books on his cases.

In a 1991 interview, Otash clarified his account of the night by saying, "Beverly Hills Police Chief Clinton Anderson once accused me of removing the knife from Stompanato's body; wiping off Lana Turner's fingerprints; putting on Cheryl Crane's fingerprints and then shoving the knife back into the body. Crazy."

When Giesler and Otash arrived at Turner's home, Lana was reportedly in tears, and Cheryl was grief stricken and in shock. Johnny Stompanato's corpse was still warm and lying in the center of Lana's bedroom. It was time to call the police. Stephen Crane took that matter into his own hands and made the call.

At about 9:40 pm. Beverly Hills Police Chief Clinton Anderson received a phone call telling him to go to 730 N. Bedford Drive immediately. "I was met outside by a man who identified himself as Stephen Crane. I asked Mr. Crane the nature of this call. Mr. Crane stated that something terrible had happened. I asked Mr. Crane if this was suicide. He said no, it was worse than that. I directly entered the residence and called the station for assistance. Following this, I went upstairs to the right and walked into the bedroom."

Chief Anderson recalled seeing "this body lying on its back with a knife wound in the upper part of the abdomen. There were two men later identified to me as Dr. Weber and Dr. McDonald. I turned to Miss Turner and asked who the victim was. She stated it was John Stompanato. I then called the station to have the detective and identification bureau men come up.

More Beverly Hills police arrived shortly after, and the press quickly got wind of the story landing on Lana's doorstep before the coroner could have the body removed. "Beverly Hills at that time was rather small; the police station was only three blocks away," Cheryl recalled.

One other person with recollections of the evening was reporter and columnist James Bacon. Bacon admitted he was there that evening, inside Lana Turner's bedroom. While his story may have been embellished over the years as a writer for *The Los Angeles Herald-Examiner*, Bacon recalled that a photographer he worked with had a police radio and phone in his car and heard a call indicating a homicide in Beverly Hills. The photographer filled Bacon in and the two men headed to 730 North Bedford in the event it turned out to be something. Bacon claimed he recognized the address as Lana's; though it's unlikely, since Turner had only recently moved into the house.

Upon arrival, the two men headed to the front door where they were stopped by police. With all his camera equipment, the photographer was barred entrance; but when they asked Bacon who he was, he simply said that he was with the coroner's office and breezed by police and into the house. Upstairs, he entered Lana's bedroom where he found the star, the body, her attorney and doctors.

"Lana was sobbing as the house soon filled up with homicide detectives," he said. "Clinton Anderson, chief of Beverly Hills police, took charge of the questioning."

Bacon said Lana told the chief, "Cheryl has killed Johnny. He threatened to kill me and poor Cherie got frightened. My poor baby. Please say that I did it. I don't want her involved. Poor baby. Please say that I did it."

Bacon said Lana repeated the last sentence to police at least a dozen times, but her lawyer told her it would be of no use trying to hide the truth and that the event, while tragic, was clearly a horrible accident. Lana still asked the chief, "Can't you arrest me instead? It was my fault. Poor baby's not to blame for all this mess."

Johnny's body is removed by the coroner.

THIRTEEN

"He kept swearing and threatening me ..."

- Lana Turner

"Actress Lana Turner's 14-year-old daughter is in jail today for stabbing to death her mother's lover, hoodlum Johnny Stompanato."

The Daily Mirror, April 5, 1958

THE POLICE STATION

Beverly Hills was still very much a small town in the late 1950s. It got its name around 1906 when Burton Green launched the Rodeo Land and Water Company, a rebranding of the Amalgamated Oil Company. Green and his wife would also rename the land it sat on as Beverly Hills, and Green would then hire the landscape architect Wilbur D. Cook to create the wide curving streets hugging the local hillside. To stimulate development, the Beverly Hills Hotel was constructed in 1912, and the city was incorporated in 1914.

The city began to get attention from the local film industry when stars like Douglas Fairbanks and Mary Pickford saw it as a place to create a larger-than-life Hollywood lifestyle of elegance. The couple built their mansion, Pickfair, in 1919 and soon other celebrities like Gloria Swanson, Will Rogers, Charlie Chaplin, Tom Mix, King Vidor, John Barrymore, Buster Keaton, Harold Lloyd, Jack Warner, Clara Bow, Harry Cohn and Rudolph Valentino followed.

The city continued to grow and by the end of World War II, Beverly Hills had become one of the most glamorous places in the world with Rodeo Drive as its centerpiece as the world's top shopping destination. By the late 1950's, little land remained and development would soon stop.

The Beverly Hills Police Department was housed within City Hall at 455 North Rexford Drive and had a small, but dependable staff to protect and serve its elite group of citizens. The station was

As Lana and Cheryl head to the police station, Johnny Stompanato's body is transported to the morgue. The press would begin gathering at the home as news of the killing spread.

just a few minutes from Lana's rental home. Around the corner, onto Santa Monica Boulevard, and up North Rodeo Drive and onto North Bedford, it would take just moments for police to make the drive that evening, even with the streets still damp from the rain earlier that night.

Lana didn't have time to think about her glamorous appearance, simply grabbing a white scarf to cover her hair, her purse, and some dark sunglasses, she and her daughter were quickly whisked away in Giesler's limousine to the nearby police station for formal questioning. While some questions were answered at the scene of the crime, Giesler wanted some extra time to work out the finer details in order for formal statements to be taken. He strategized with Lana and Cheryl in the car ride over. Due to the sequence of events, rumors would begin circulating almost immediately that Lana had killed her lover and was using Cheryl to cover up the crime.

Arriving at the Beverly Hills Police Station along with Police Chief Anderson, Cheryl was led to an interview room for the first of several formal questionings about the incidents of April 4. With her mother present, Cheryl recounted the tragic events from a few hours earlier in her own words, with the help of Police Captain Ray Borders.

"Tell us just what happened," asked Detective Borders.

"Well, they had an argument; then he was threatening Mother."

"How?" he asked.

"Well, to kill her and hurt Daddy, Gran and me."

"He threatened to hurt all of you?

"Yes," said Cheryl.

"How?"

"He said he had ways of doing it."

"Where was this argument taking place?

"First, in my bedroom and then in Mother's room," Cheryl

answered.

Detective Borders had Cheryl recount what she could hear and interpret from the arguments inside her mother's bedroom and eventually led her to the moment of the killing.

"He kept threatening her and I thought he was going to hurt her, so I rushed into the room and struck him with the knife. He screamed and asked me what I was doing. I ran out of the room," Cheryl said. "Mother called me back and said to help her. Finally, I came back. I called Daddy before I went back in the first time, and I told him to come over fast."

Chief Anderson, who was also in attendance for the questioning, next turned to Lana, "Well, now Miss Turner, you heard your daughter's version of this incident. Would it be better if we talked to you without her being present?"

Lana answered immediately, "No, She can stay. Everything she said is true. It started out as more or less a teasing thing about his age, as my daughter mentioned, and then from there it just began as one more lie on top of the other; but it was still pleasant enough that it was not vicious. And then just one word after the other. And I went into my daughter's room where she was watching television and he walked in after me and continued the argument in front of her."

Lana explained that the argument escalated, but she wasn't aware of how much Cheryl had heard or understood. "I am not sure how long Cheryl was outside the door. I know that when I opened it at one point she was there."

"Then she came into the room?" asked Chief Anderson.

"She just came inside the door, and the door was open. He was standing there with a jacket and shirt over his shoulder and he kept on and on with these threats, and Cheryl said, 'John, don't talk to mother like that.' And I think he said, 'I will talk to her or anyone else.'"

Lana continued, "And he went on and even more viciously verbally. The next thing I knew – this sounds strange – it happened so fast – it did, and I truthfully thought Cheryl had just poked him in the stomach. And then he pulled away from her."

The questioning went on from there, with questions to Cheryl and then back to Lana about the sequence of events, what was said by whom, and what was done over the course of the evening.

Eventually, after roughly two hours, the formal statements were taken and the questioning exhausted, Lana and Stephen Crane asked the authorities to release Cheryl into their hands or into the custody of their lawyer Jerry Giesler. The request was rejected. Cheryl was formally charged with the killing and led away to spend

Lana and her lawyer leaving the Beverly Hills police station with Lana in tears and Cheryl behind bars.

the rest of the evening in the Beverly Hills jail. Lana was assured that Cheryl would receive the best of care and she and her ex-husband were allowed then to leave. They planned to return in the morning to check on their daughter.

Meanwhile, the media was beginning to gather outside Lana's new home hoping to catch a glimpse of some of the drama unfolding. Police photographed the scene; collected all the evidence and loaded Stompanato's body onto a gurney, covered by a white sheet.

Police sources reportedly tipped off the media and by morning, crime scene photos of Stompanato and Lana Turner made front-page headlines on nearly every newspaper in the country.

Camera flashes ignited the nighttime skies on Bedford Drive when the door to Lana's home opened and officers of the county coroner carried out the body of Johnny Stompanato onto the brick driveway and into an awaiting black Dodge coroner's van. Stompanato was transported to the morgue for an autopsy. Police stood guard at Lana's front door in the event any press made another attempt to sneak their way inside.

At police headquarters, as Cheryl was placed into custody, they went by the book. "I think that they were so careful to make sure they dotted all their 'I's and crossed all their T's," Cheryl recalled years later. "And they didn't want anyone to show they showed favoritism, you know, a star's kid or anything like that, because they kept me overnight at the Beverly Hills Police Station in a cell."

At about the same time, Mickey Cohen was called to identify Johnny Stompanato's body at the morgue. As his employer and friend, Cohen was the one who actually helped Stompanato get access to Lana's private phone numbers. It was through his connections that Johnny was so adept at keeping track of Lana's whereabouts, including who she was seeing and often where she was headed. However, Cohen wasn't doing it out of the goodness of his heart. He thought he might one day be able to use the details of her affair with Johnny to his own benefit – and was all to willing to blackmail her if necessary. Now, with Johnny Stompanato dead, he tried to look at how he could turn the tragic events to his own benefit.

Publicly, he first played his cards close to his vest. "I can't understand it," Mickey told the press. "I thought she liked him very much. We were happy Cheryl and Johnny and me. We used to go horseback riding together," he claimed.

After his trip to the morgue, he told reporters, "I don't like the whole thing. There's lots of unanswered questions ... I'm going to find some of those answers no matter what happens."

By morning, the media storm was in full swing. While news of Bob Hope announcing plans to write a book about his recent trips to Russia, and MGM pulling out all the stops to promote *Ben-Hur*, might have dominated headlines that morning; newspaper front pages were pulled and reset with headlines that Lana Turner's daughter had killed her mother's lover. Once the story went out over the wires, newspapers across the U.S. and abroad would be covering the biggest Hollywood story of the century.

Headlines in newspapers around the world would chronicle the
events surrounding Johnny's death for weeks after the stabbing.

FOURTEEN

"The best I can remember, they
came together and they parted."
- Lana Turner

"The papers loved the story and the coroner's inquest was one of the most sensational legal hearings Hollywood has ever seen. Turner's tale on the stand was riveting: a wayward mother in distress and the faithful daughter who comes to her rescue."

Time Magazine, 2007

THE MEDIA STORM

The media had a field day with what they called a "gossip-strewn romance between the one-time sweater girl and the dark-haired former underworld figure who had squired her here, in London and in Acapulco, Mexico."

What started out suddenly as a case of an accidental stabbing took off in a host of directions. At first, the story centered on the killing itself, reports like, "The body of Johnny Stompanato, clad in dark slacks, a sweater and a gray jacket, remained on the floor of the upstairs bedroom where the stabbing occurred," were just the tip of the iceberg in the first days following the killing. And the media ate it up when it came out that police found a photo of Lana, bearing an affectionate inscription from the star in Johnny's personal belongings he had with him the night he died."

Newspaper reports detailed how Cheryl came home from school, "expecting a merry Easter vacation from the Happy Valley School at Ojai." But how the innocence was shattered that "very night she returned she heard a stormy battle between Stompanato and her mother and listened in childish terror at the invective and threats that volleyed through the house."

Lana Turner's Daughter Slays Gangster Boy Friend of Mother

"DID IT TO PROTECT MY MOTHER"—Cheryl Crane (left), and her mother, Lana Turner (right), in Hollywood yesterday after the fourteen-year-old girl killed Miss Turner's gangster boy friend.

The press would cover every aspect of the case for weeks.

Reports then began to look deeper into who the victim was. They painted Johnny as a thug, calling him "the dapper Adonis of the underworld. His checkered past had him described, "often as the escort of older women, usually wealthy." Stompanato was also called a member of a bad crowd referred as, "Mickey Cohen and his 40 thieves."

Cheryl's past then came into focus as well, after reporters found out that she ran away from home not long prior because she didn't want to attend a private school in Flintridge. Reports said "a man found her on skid row and took her to the Hollenbeck Police Station where she was reunited with her parents."

Lana's relationship with Johnny would also become a major focus for the press, digging up anything they could on the couple from the past year. This included Lana's fearing for her life, including the claim that, "On occasion John said he would cut my face with a razor," Lana was documented as saying in police reports.

If that weren't enough, Mickey Cohen had his own stories to spin, as well as his own legal troubles. On April 8 - the same day much of the dirt was hitting the newsstands, Mickey Cohen was found guilty of hitting a waiter, *The Los Angeles Times* made it front page news, alongside Lana's drama. The incident dated back to an altercation on January 29 in which the crime boss slugged a waiter at Villa Capri restaurant.

Meanwhile, Carmine Stompanato, Johnny's older brother, arrived in Hollywood on April 5 to claim his brother's body. Carmine Stompanato was called "soft-spoken," but "a tired, defeated looking man."

At 45, he was just a few years senior to Johnny, but was called on by the family to bring their brother and son home. *The Los Angeles Times* saw him as a man out of his element as he "patiently tries to unravel the red tape of official processes." Aside from claim-

ing his brother's body, he had to cope with what remained of Johnny's estate and affairs, all while the media circled around his every
move.

Mickey Cohen reportedly tried to claim the body and personal effects, but was "spurned by the coroner's office, which said
the family would have to take charge." Once Carmine Stompanato
arrived, they were able to arrange for Johnny to be released from
the morgue in an inexpensive coffin. Carmine told reporters that he
would transport his body to Woodstock, Illinois for a burial planned

Mickey Cohen would see that Johnny got a Los Angeles funeral service before heading to Illinois for burial.

for Wednesday and a service at the Thomas Merwins Mortuary.

Before leaving the state, Johnny would first be given a service in Los Angeles at the Godeau Martinoni Mortuary. A grief-stricken Carmine was overheard by reporters mumbling, "I don't want to see him this way." At the service, scores of Johnny's friends – including a number of his local organized crime contacts – came to pay their respects before he was shipped off to Illinois. Carmine was perplexed by the turn of events, "It just doesn't seem possible he would just stand there and let somebody put a knife into him."

After the killing, Lana moved out of the house on Bedford Drive and rented another home on nearby Canyon Drive, she focused her attention on the inquest unfolding before her; her need to explain the situation and preventing Cheryl from paying the price for Lana's mistake of allowing Johnny Stompanato into their lives.

Carmine announced his plans to return home "after trying in vain to obtain an audience with Lana." Shortly after the Los Angeles service, Johnny was sent home to Woodstock, Illinois where he was buried after another small service. He was interred in Oakland Cemetery in McHenry County, between his mother, Carmela, who died in 1925 and his father John who died in 1952. Lana did not attend either service for Johnny.

Carmine continued to vent his frustrations with Hollywood. He told reporters that he was "far from satisfied with the film star's version of his brother's death and that it had been suggested to him that she be given a lie detector test."

"I don't have any desire to prosecute this girl (Cheryl)," said Carmine. "I just want the truth to come out. There have been a lot of lies printed."

Carmine also told the press that he denied Miss Turner's statement that Stompanato chased her to Europe last year. The truth, he said, "was that the movie star sent his brother a ticket to join her."

Meanwhile, Johnny's stepmother angrily said his "name is being slandered" by Lana and the press, and "they are saying things that couldn't be possible. An American flag was draped across the foot of his coffin for his service in the military.

Not long after the Stompanato's death, one of Lana's attorneys, Louis Blau, arrived at her home with a package of film negatives showing a naked, sleeping Lana Turner. Johnny had reportedly taken them. The attorney acquired them through Lana's maid, Arminda. She has supposedly been given an envelope by Stompanato shortly before he left to meet Lana in England, telling her the contents were "extremely valuable to him." She was asked keep it safe until he was able to reclaim it. Arminda reportedly never opened the package, but rather locked it in the trunk of her car and simply forgot about it. Stompanato never returned to her to collect the package, and it wasn't until after his death that she recalled having it. She gave it to

Johnny would be buried in Woodstock, Illinois in a family service. Lana would not attend his funeral.

Lana's lawyer, so he could determine if it held any importance in the case.

In addition to the pictures of Lana, other shots showed Stompanato having sex with another woman. Lana's attorney suspected that the shots could be put together in such a way to put Lana in a very compromising position. "He could hold them over you for blackmail," Lana's attorney said. Lana later wrote in her autobiography that she suspected Stompanato may have drugged her one afternoon with a drink and took the photos without her knowledge, with the intent to use them against her one day.

Lana burned the negatives and flushed the ashes down the toilet. Had Mickey Cohen gotten his hands on the photographs, it would have been very ugly for Lana. Even though he lost the photos Cohen knew Johnny had kept love letters which he and Lana had exchanged during the past year. He had one of his henchmen break into Johnny's apartment, locate the letters and bring them to him.

A rainstorm came just in time for Easter, but for the Turners and Cranes, the weather was a blur, as was the Easter holiday. Deputy District Attorney Manley Bowler told the press Cheryl would be "treated no different than any other girl. She will be booked like any other juvenile and will be kept in Beverly Hills jail overnight."

Cheryl was formally booked as a juvenile offender a short time later and spent the next few nights – and coming weeks – in detention, locked away from her mother while authorizes tried to piece together the lurid details that got her there. She reportedly remarked, "I'm pretty strong - stronger than mother is," but added, "I wish I could be like my mother. I wish I could cry."

Lana and her ex-husband received special permission to visit their daughter that Easter, arriving at the electronic gates of Juvenile Hall in two Cadillacs where they were ushered in to see their daughter while other parents waited for the usual 1 pm visiting hour.

On Monday morning, Cheryl was brought before a probate judge for the pre-detention hearing. Both sides of the case were permitted to address the court, and Jerry Giesler told the judge he could prove Stompanato's death was justifiable homicide, requesting that Cheryl be released to her grandmother's custody. "Lana's daughter acted out of extreme fear of Stompanato," said Giesler, adding that she "obviously struck at him in an attempt to defend her mother from an attack which had been repeatedly threatened by Stompanato."

News reports spilled out whatever facts they had been told. "Dapper Johnny Stompanato, 42, constant companion of film star Lana Turner, was stabbed to death last night by Lana's 14-year old daughter, Cheryl, after Stompanato, ex-mobster assertedly threatened the actress. Disclosure that the only child of the actress killed Miss Turner's constant companion of recent months was made by Police Chief Clinton Anderson after the daughter, Miss Turner and Stephen Crane, former husband of Lana and father of the girl, had been closeted for nearly two hours in the Beverly Hills Police Station."

Police told reporters he was "stabbed in the right side with a 10-inch butcher knife." Police Chief Anderson, when interviewed, said "It seems that Stompanato had long been unwelcome in the Turner home and resisted every effort of Miss Turner to discourage his attention and leave the house."

Police reports suggested that Lana had told Stompanato that she wanted to be rid of him. "He threatened to maim her, to disfigure her, and to beat her."

Lana also told Anderson about Stompanato's assault on her after the Oscars weeks earlier. It was noted in the reports as "a severe beating to her with his fists."

Meanwhile, Sean Connery - learning of Stompanato's death - was warned to lay low due his encounter with Stompanato on the set of *Another Time, Another Place*. He went into hiding after hearing a rumor that Mickey Cohen and others were spreading the word that

Johnny's killing was related to Connery's rumored affair with Lana. Connery reportedly was told that Mickey Cohen warned him, "Get out of town or a contract will be put on your life."

Fearing that the mobster wanted anybody involved in the murder killed he checked out of the Hollywood Roosevelt Hotel where he was staying and relocated to a small guesthouse outside

Lana arrives in court alongside her lawyer Jerry Giesler.

LA until the drama blew over. He avoided contact with Lana and worried about his own life. He also worried about his career and next move role. He had been cast in Walt Disney's next big picture, *Darby O'Gill and the Little People.* Connery feared that if details of a rumored affair and role in the Stompanato scandal hit the newspapers, he'd be fired because the salacious details didn't fit into Disney's wholesome family image. Connery kept a low profile and held onto his job. It was Lana whose career had the most to lose.

Even though Johnny was gone, his presence was ever present for Lana in the days that followed the tragedy. It would turn out to be Hollywood's biggest media circus in decades. And while Lana was quite familiar with seeing her name in print, the drama that would unfold following the death of Johnny Stompanato was at times more than even she could handle. The salacious details of not only the crime, but also the torrid love affair she found herself trapped in, became fodder for every newspaper and media organization around the world. Lana's version of events had her trapped in an abusive relationship where she felt she had no way out. While it made for good headlines, it wasn't entirely the truth. It was true that Stompanato had a dark side and Lana may genuinely have felt fear during the affair, but she too found herself drawn to him. And Mickey Cohen knew it.

Cohen wasn't about to let Lana play herself as a victim in this drama and make Johnny out to be some cruel hoodlum who tortured and abused her. He leaked the love letters he had stolen to the press, and *The Los Angeles Herald Examiner* was the first to break the story.

"A pack of letters – possibly Lana Turner's purported purple love missives to Johnny Stompanato – mysteriously disappeared from his apartment on the very night he was stabbed to death in the actress' home, West Hollywood Police learned yesterday."

Police took a burglary report from the owner of the building who said a shaving kit with a pack of letters had supposedly been removed from the apartment sometime between 2:30 p.m. Good Friday and 6 a.m. Saturday morning.

It was just two days before the inquest when the newspaper reprinted every word of Johnny's letters to Lana and hers back to him. The 12 letters provided a deep and intimate look at Lana and Johnny's relationship. Lana called her dead lover "My Dearest Darling, Love," "Honey Pot," "Darling Papito," and "Daddy Darling."

In the steamy letters at the beginning of the affair, there was talk of "our love, our hopes, our dreams, our sex and longings." Later, they showed Lana's pleas for space towards the end writing, "You must let me alone in my 'own world' for a while, to rest, think, rest, think." Lana's affair was exposed to the world.

Mickey Cohen admitted he leaked the letters, saying, "I thought it was fair to show that Johnny wasn't exactly 'unwelcome company' like Lana said," he told *The Herald Examiner.*

The publishing of the letters was also raised as a risk at getting to the truth. Louis Lyons, curator of the Neiman Fellowships for Journalism at Harvard University slammed the press for publishing the lurid letters, saying, "What chance would there be to select a jury uninfluenced by this prejudicial material that is splattered across the land?"

Adding that the letters were not part of any court proceeding and may have been gained through theft or profit, he said that the letters were intended to damage Lana, but could very well cloud the case of facts in the actual death of Johnny Stompanato.

In truth, the letters did imply that Lana had not been as fearful of Johnny as she claimed to police. Even after the incidents in London, Lana wrote to Johnny after his departure saying, "So may precious things you told me, described to me, each beautiful and intimate detail of our love, our hopes, our dreams, our sex and longings. ... My God, how you could write and when near me, make most of those dreams come to life with the realness of you and me and us ..."

Lana received a bit good press when *The Los Angeles Times* got hold of Ted Stauffer, manager and part owner of Via Vera Hotel, the plush villa where Lana and Johnny stayed on their last visit to Acapulco. Stauffer told the news journal that the pair had separate suites, and that he sensed "Lana's apparent uneasiness."

"He wouldn't let her alone for a minute," said Stauffer. "I got the impression that Lana was worried, because she knew she had gotten herself into something; decided she didn't like it; and didn't know how to get out."

Ted Stauffer had actually become friends with Lana over the years. Having once been married to actress Hedy Lamarr, Stauffer was the man who gave Lana the nickname "Lanita," and she nearly always stayed at his villa when visiting.

Stauffer believed Lana intended to vacation there alone, until Johnny managed to insert himself into the trip. "She wrote to me from London last December to reserve the bungalow she always has here," said Stauffer. "And I think – at that time, at least – she planned to be alone, because in her letter, she wrote that it would be strange for her to be in Acapulco alone. Before, she has always been with a husband and her family."

Stauffer explained that three days before Lana arrived, he received a call from Stompanato who stated that he would be accompanying her on her visit. "He was tough," he said. " He gave me orders I couldn't take."

However, with each bit of good news came more troubles. In addition to the release of her love letters and the issue with the photos Johnny had hid from her, Lana found also other troubling details. He kept a "little brown book" filled with the phone numbers of many prominent Hollywood women, including Zsa Zsa Gabor, Anita Eckberg, June Allyson, Janet Leigh, Ava Gardner, as well as a number of notable men. Also among Johnny's personal effects were a collection of letters from creditors showing Stompanato was buried in debt, including one bar bill for $900 bearing his name along with Lana's.

The Los Angeles Times reportedly got wind of the tan leather address book, "replete with some of Hollywood's top names and phone numbers." One of the owners of the complex where Johnny lived reportedly opened his apartment looking for "a will or other personal papers" and discovered the notebook during his search.

Johnny's apartment at the Del Capri Hotel became a place of interest for reporters. "Strewn with magazines and newspapers," the press knew people had managed to work their way through the place searching for dirt, much of it scooped up by Mickey Cohen and his gang. Reporters did note that Johnny had a love of sports clothes, "according to an inspection of his closet," which showed a wide collection of expensive sport coats and "three smartly tailored suits on individual hangers."

Newsmen detailed the state of Johnny's apartment that consisted of a living room with combination bar and kitchen, a bedroom with twin beds, and a bathroom. What they found most interesting was a suitcase, not yet unpacked, that bore plane tags with a departure from London, most likely from his ill-fated trip to visit Lana during the filming of *Another Time, Another Place.*

While the media scooped up every detail surrounding Johnny and Lana's relationship, his checkered past, and the impending court proceeding, Lana still wasn't speaking. Other than the references in police reports, the media and public had not heard Lana's side of the story. And while many of the facts seemed clear, everyone still wanted to hear it from Lana. Rumors even circulated that Lana had caught Johnny in bed with Cheryl and killed him in a crime of passion, but rumors were all they were.

By April 9 it was clear that Lana was going to have to take the stand at the coroner's inquest to get her story on the record and in front of the media. She'd done her best to avoid speaking to the press. Her lawyers helped her remain as low-profile as possible. On April 10, the media reported that Lana would in fact take the stand on the 11th. "Miss Turner, who has been in seclusion except to visit her daughter in juvenile hall, will be the star witness today when a coroner's inquest convenes at 9 a.m. in the Hall of Records."

The Los Angeles Times reported that "Beverly Hills Police Chief Clinton H. Anderson paid an 11th hour visit to actress Lana Turner last night, as Lana prepared to deliver the most important lines of her career – a recital of the moments of horror a week ago when her 14-year-old daughter Cheryl took the life of Johnny Stompanato.

Anderson reportedly asked Lana if she were going to testify and she replied she would. Cheryl, being a minor, would not.

Newspapers around the country had Lana Tuner on the front pages for weeks after the stabbing. Everyone waited to hear her side of the story in court.

FIFTEEN

*"I was walking toward the bed-
room door and he was right
behind me, and I opened it, and
my daughter came in."*

- Lana Turner

"The cracking emotion of a near-riotous inquest was climaxed in tears and spectator applause yesterday as the coroner's jury ruled ..."

The Los Angeles Time, April 11, 1958

THE INQUEST OPENS

While attention was something Lana had long coveted, her name splashed across every newspaper front-page in the country, and her daughter being labeled a murderess, were difficult to see. She'd never expected to be handed a mother of the year award, but the news of her romancing a gangster before the eyes of her daughter, made some question her parenting skills and choices.

Lana, with the help of attorney Jerry Giesler, wasn't about to go down without a fight. She used the invasion of privacy as another chance to present herself as a victim. The mob was out to destroy her. Her daughter was only protecting her - from both herself as well as Johnny. Some would call the inquest "Lana's greatest performance," and the media and public ate up the gossip and lurid details.

One of Lana's smartest moves was in obtaining the help of Jerry Giesler in defending both her and her daughter as the nightmare unfolded. Giesler had made a name for himself throughout Hollywood by the late 1950s.

Born in 1886, Harold Lee "Jerry" Giesler arrived in Los Angeles in 1907 to attend law school at the University of Southern California. He found the concepts of law fascinating, but dropped out of school around 1909, choosing to study with renowned attorney Earl Rogers and earn his law degree through real case work. By 1910 he was admitted to the bar, practicing under the name, "H. L. Giesler." He assisted Rogers in the defense of the nation's top criminal defense attorney, Clarence Darrow, during one of his early cases.

Jerry Giesler would eventually become one of the highest paid attorneys in his field by defending many of Hollywood's biggest talents. The case that put him on the map came in 1929 when Alexander Pantages, a motion picture producer and owner of one of the largest film theater chains in the U.S., was arrested and charged with the rape of 17-year-old Eunice Pringle, an aspiring vaudeville dancer. She claimed that Pantages had attacked her in a closet in his downtown theater after she auditioned for him.

The sensational case garnered a large amount of news coverage that mostly presented Pantages as a monster. On October 27, 1929 he was convicted and sentenced to 50 years in prison, but he continued to claim the whole case was a set up. Jerry Giesler was hired to file an appeal and to petition the court for a new trial. The California Supreme Court agreed to hear the case.

In a shrewd maneuver, Giesler put Eunice Pringle's character on trial and presented Pringle as a woman of low morals. He convinced the court that rape would have been nearly impossible in Pantages' broom closet and raised questions over how a young athletic actress was unable to fight off the 54-year-old Pantages, who was only 5-feet-6-and-a-half inches tall. The jury dismissed the case and Pantages won acquittal in 1931.

The case put Giesler at the top of a short list of go-to Hollywood lawyers, and soon everyone was calling on him for assistance. Errol Flynn hired him to successfully earn an acquittal on charges of

Cheryl Crane arrives for one of the numerous court proceedings.

statutory rape. Marilyn Monroe hired him for her divorce from Joe DiMaggio. Other famous clients included actor Robert Mitchum, Charlie Chaplin, gangster Bugsy Siegel, and producer Walter Wanger, who was accused of shooting Hollywood agent Jennings Lang after finding out he was having an affair with Wanger's wife, actress Joan Bennett.

In 1958, Giesler was being summoned again. This time it was to defend 14-year-old Cheryl Crane, daughter of a movie star. With the case heavily publicized around the world, it was just the sort of case the lawyer lived for.

Two days after the homicide, Los Angeles County District Attorney William B. McKesson held a press conference, saying in no uncertain terms "would the case receive special treatment simply because movie star Lana Turner was involved." Cheryl, who had been held overnight in the Beverly Hills jail, was remanded to the county Juvenile Hall and remained there until the case was resolved. Even though criminal charges had not yet been filed against the teen, Cheryl was held as a material witness and adjudicated as a juvenile. Due to the nature of the crime, more serious charges loomed over her.

Easter Sunday came and went and on Monday morning Cheryl appeared before a probate judge for a pre-detention hearing. Prosecutors and her defense attorney each were permitted to address the court. Giesler told the judge that he could prove Stompanato's death was justifiable homicide. Arthur Crowley, a lawyer hired by Stephen Crane, petitioned the court to have Cheryl released to her grandmother, but the request was denied.

Fortunately for Lana and Cheryl, the police chief was on their side and didn't see any cover-up behind their story. "Let's go to trial," said Beverly Hills Police Chief William Anderson. "I am satisfied that Stompanato was killed with a knife, and we have the party who did it."

The district attorney recommended that Cheryl not be released on bail. He was afraid that the mob or Lana Turner would pressure Cheryl one way or another. The judge agreed and ordered Cheryl detained in Juvenile Hall. The judge then ordered, against the recommendations of the police and the district attorney's office, that a coroner's inquest be held to determine whether a crime had actually been committed.

During a coroner's inquest, a jury, selected by the coroner, examines the circumstances surrounding a suspicious death and renders a verdict. While the verdict may or may not identify the person or persons responsible for a death, it aims to determine cause of death. Juries may recommend further investigation and assign blame to negligent parties. Unlike grand jury indictments, the verdict from a coroner's inquest is not binding. Law enforcement officials may still levy charges, depending on their preference. An inquest can be helpful to the court by formally establishing the cause of death and any important circumstances, including if a crime were actually committed. It also can provide prosecutors with the oppor-

Mickey Cohen was one of the first people called to testify during the inquest, but he had little to say, fearing he'd be implicated in Johnny's death.

193

tunity to see how evidence influences jurors before deciding to try a case. In the death of Johnny Stompanato, the inquest was set for Friday, April 11, nearly one week since the incident occurred.

After the hearing, Steven Crane was asked by the press if he were aware of his ex-wife's longtime romance with the LA mobster. He answered simply, "No." He also told them that he had no intention of trying to have Lana declared an unfit mother or to try obtaining full custody of his daughter. "Despite all this, I believe Lana is a loving, good mother."

As news of the coming inquest got around town, Carmine Stompanato was frustrated at not being able to act as a voice for Johnny. He felt the case was becoming a smear campaign against his brother, and there was little he could do about it. "I'm at a dead end, and I can't afford to fight three people, She (Miss Turner) has got more money, one of the greatest lawyers in the world and the Chief of Police of Beverly Hills California working for her. … How am I going to fight Giesler and the movie colony?"

The media also managed to get Johnny's mother to open up more with her claiming that Lana was not so against the idea of marrying her son and that Lana had even considered sending Cheryl to public school in Johnny's hometown under an assumed name. She said that she burned all the letters she had received from her son. When asked why, she claimed it was because they were damaging. "To whom," they asked, and she replied, "Miss Turner."

Inside the Hall of Records in downtown Beverly Hills the largest courtroom was reserved for the coroner's inquest. Of the 160 seats in the courtroom, 120 were reserved for the press. CBS and ABC announced that they were going to broadcast the inquest live, and radio stations planned to broadcast it as well.

By 6 am., a line had formed outside the Beverly Hills Hall of Records for the scant 40 public seats not set aside for the media. Just before 9 am., television cameras rolled and flashbulbs went off as

Lana, Stephen Crane and Lana's mother Mildred, and Jerry Giesler, made their way up the courthouse steps and into the building. They took their seats in the courtroom, and the whispers and energy quieted down as the judge entered and the inquest began.

Jerry Giesler managed to get Cheryl excused from having to testify due to the trauma she had already been through. Cheryl would attend the hearing, wearing a white polo coat along with a solemn face. Reporters noted that she did not cry during the pro-

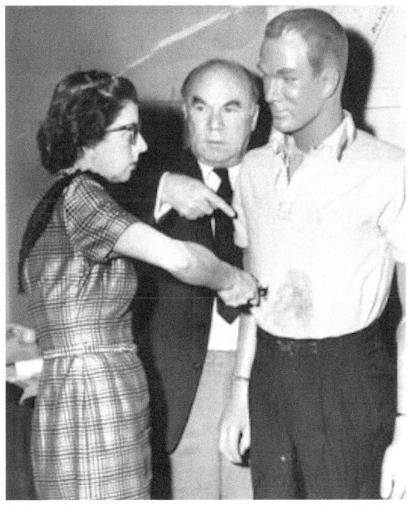

A dramatic court moment came in a reenactment of the killing.

ceedings though both her parents did.

Policemen who were at the scene that evening, along with medical personnel, were called to testify; but as far as the court and media were concerned, there was only one real witness whose testimony was key to getting to the truth. Lana Tuner was the only person who saw Cheryl stab Johnny Stompanato, and everyone wanted to hear what the star had to say.

Los Angeles mob kingpin Mickey Cohen was the first person called to testify, having first identified Johnny's body at the morgue. Cohen only spent a couple minutes on the stand. Questioned by

Johnny Stompanato's death certificate.

Deputy Coroner Charles C. Langhauser and identified as Michael Cohen, he stated his name as Mickey Cohen and was asked if he had "reviewed the remains of the deceased person in this matter."

"I reviewed some remains, yes." Cohen replied.

"Was that somebody you had known in life?" asked Langhauser.

"I refuse to identify the body," he answered.

"Did you make a statement that the deceased person was John Stompanato Jr.?", Langhauser continued.

"I refuse to identify him as John Stompanato Jr. on the grounds that I may be accused of this murder," responded Cohen, who was then quickly excused from further testimony. Mickey Cohen, who had spent his fair share of time in a courtroom, quickly left the building.

Mickey Cohen was gone by the time the coroner introduced the autopsy report and testified that "a whole team of doctors" could not have saved John Stompanato's life. Though Johnny was stabbed only once in the abdomen, the knife sliced one of his kidneys, struck a vertebra and then twisted upward, puncturing his aorta. He died within a matter of minutes. The medical examiner then surprised everyone by stating that the autopsy revealed that the victim probably would not have lived another 10 years due to his bad liver.

Several police officers were called to testify about the recollections of the events that night. Questions around who was in the home at the time of the events; what time specific activities occurred, and the state of the house after the killing were the major topics.

Deputy District Attorney William McGinley looked for signs of a cover-up when inquiring about the scene of the crime that evening. During questioning, McGinley took the first police officer on the scene back to the evening of April 4 and asked him what he recalled. "After you arrived at the premises, I believe you went up to the bedroom and saw the body of a male person; is that right?" asked

McGinley.

"That's correct," he replied.

"Did you notice any blood on the that person?"

"No, there was no blood that I saw on the person. There was a bloody towel."

"There was a bloody towel?" McGinley confirmed.

"Yes," said the officer.

"Where was the bloody towel?"

"It was to the right of the body."

"On the rug?"

"Yes, it was."

"Did you see any blood there in the room, on any of the furniture, or on the rug or anything like that?"

"No, I did not."

"Did you notice any of the furniture knocked over?"

"No, sir."

McGinley next brought Chief Anderson to the stand to discuss his involvement in the events that evening, focusing on the murder weapon.

"Did you see Cheryl Crane that evening?", asked McGinley.

"In her bedroom, yes," replied Anderson.

"What was her condition emotionally, could you tell us about that?"

"I would say she was in shock, upset."

"Did you notice any blood on her clothing or the body of either Lana Turner or Cheryl or the knife?"

"Yes. The knife."

"Where did you first see the knife?"

"It was in a bathroom adjacent to the bedroom laying on a stand."

"Chief Anderson, I will show you a regular type of butcher knife which has stains on it. Would you please examine that and tell us if you have ever seen it before?"

"I have."

"Is that the knife that you saw in the bathroom that evening?"

"Yes."

"Now, the red stains that are on the knife, did they appear to be moist at that time, or were they dry as they appear now?"

"No, they were moist."

Discussion of the knife and blood would continue, as prosecutors tried to show that a lack of blood may have implied a clean up of the scene before police arrived.

"Was the scientific examination made of the knife by your crime lab?"

"It was."

"What were the results of the examination by the crime lab?"

"There was a smudged fingerprint, but not enough points for identification," responded Anderson.

"Chief Anderson, did you notice the occasion of any spots of blood or smears of blood on any of the furniture or rugs in the bedroom?"

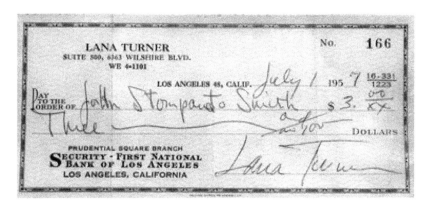

Even checks written to Johnny from Lana were used in court to show Johnny profiting from his relationship with the star.

"I remember seeing three blood spots about the size of a 10-cent piece alongside the body."

"Alongside the body?"

"Yes"

"The body was lying on the floor?"

"Laying on his back, yes."

"Arms outstretched?"

"They were along each side [indicating]."

Anderson was then asked about the doctors at the scene and victim in the bedroom.

"How was John Stompanato Jr. dressed when you first saw him that evening?"

"Well, when I arrived he had his pants and shirt on and his shirt was turned up and I could see the wound on his stomach."

"Were any doctors operating on him at the time or had there been just before you got there?" asked McGinley.

"As I arrived," began Anderson. Transcripts note an additional part of his response, but it is inaudible.

McGinley continued. "Did you see a Dr. McDonald and a Dr. Weber there?

Anderson replied, "Dr. McDonald was in the room and I later saw Dr. Weber,

Chief Anderson was also questioned about his taking testimony from both Cheryl and Lana before leaving the scene of the crime. When asked about Cheryl's words that evening, he said that she said, "I stabbed him. I didn't mean to kill him – I just meant to frighten him."

The courtroom took a recess and when it returned, the star witness was ready to testify.

Lana and Mildred Turner arrive with lawyers and press at the inquest in April 1958.

SIXTEEN

"Don't ... don't ever touch me again.
I am ... I am absolutely finished!"
                                                    - Lana Turner

"The actress testified for an hour - haltingly, constantly on the brink of collapse - and told of the horror-filled moments last Friday when her "baby" plunged the knife into Stompanato's stomach."

The Los Angeles Times, April 12, 1958

LANA TAKES THE STAND

At last, the media, district attorney, defense and the public inside the packed courtroom would have a chance to hear it from the only eyewitness. It was Lana Turner's chance to tell her story to the 10-man, two-woman jury. She had never felt such intense pressure to deliver on a performance. Lana was not a stage actor. She wasn't particularly comfortable in front of an audience, but knew what it was like to be in front of a crowd, and she enjoyed being the center of attention.

But it was different this time. She had the need to tell the story that people wanted to hear - and in a way that made it clear and believable what had happened. The night of April 4 was a horrible mistake. At stake was her daughter's future.

The coroner's inquest into the death of Johnny Stompanato wasn't just about those in attendance. It turned out to be the most anticipated television event of its time. Broadcast live on CBS and ABC and going out live on radio as well, it was the real thing and without a movie set, and viewers wanted to hear her story.

Dressed in a conservative gray silk suit, she stepped forward onto the witness stand for what was already an uncomfortable day. She removed her matching hat and was ready to deliver her testimony. Her platinum hair wasn't movie-star perfect, and she had barely slept the night before, but the subtle makeup was enough. Even under difficult circumstances Lana Turner was still a beautiful woman.

She took to the witness stand, sat down, removed the white glove from her left hand, leaving the right glove on, clutching a handkerchief, and took a deep breath.

"State your name."

"Lana Turner."

"Your address."

"730 North Bedford Drive, Beverly Hills."

From then on, speaking softly, she tried to explain the sequence of events.

For the next hour, Lana answered questions from the coroner, his deputy and her own lawyer, Jerry Giesler, while the jurors watched intently. She rarely made eye contact with her questioners, instead staring at the back of the courtroom where the wall met the ceiling. Through the entire testimony, she only referred to the victim as Mr. Stompanato.

She had to answer why she stayed with a man who beat her, something she didn't herself understand. Under Giesler's questioning, she provided a moment-by-moment recount of the argument that led to the Johnny's stabbing. She broke down twice on the stand. Lana's 62-minute testimony recounted her version of the events and the abusive relationship with Stompanato. "Mr. Stompanato grabbed my arm, shook me," she testified. "[He] said, as he told me before, no matter what I did or how I tried to get away he would never let me."

Lana breaks down during her testimony on the witness stand.

According to her testimony, the night began to unravel when she learned he had been lying to her about his age. It was one of the many lies she claimed he had told her, and she said it would be the last lie as well. She told him she was ending it. She said that she went upstairs and then into Cheryl's room where she was doing schoolwork and watching television, and Johnny followed. It was a little past 8 p.m. and Lana remembered the time distinctly.

"I happened to glance at the TV and I remembered, that it was *The Phil Silvers Show* and I had been out of the country for a number of months working and I had not seen TV, so I was hoping that I would be able to watch it for a moment, but he continued saying these things and I finally turned to him and I said, 'I have told you and told you I do not want to argue with you in front of the baby.' – I have always called her that, and he said he didn't know why the – why not. I said, 'Well, we are not going to.' So, I turned directly to my daughter and I said, 'I am going downstairs, I am coming right back up. I am going to my room.' I don't know why I said that."

Lana explained that Cheryl remained in her room watching TV, but Johnny followed her downstairs. "… The quarreling now becoming more violent – and – I , I – I was just finding out too many lies, and that this one was one more that I found out was just not the worst lie. But it was one that, no matter what made me say to him, 'I can't go on like this, you know that I have begged, I have pleaded for you to leave me alone,' even with all of the threats, which I admit I had great fear of him."

His voice grew louder and his threats of violence escalated with Cheryl listening as the two came back upstairs and into her mother's room.

Twisting her hands as she answered, she recalled the next horrific, fateful moments. She closed her eyes, touched at her face and continued. "He grabbed me by the arms and started shaking me and cursing me very badly, and saying that, as he had told me before, no matter what I did, how I tried to get away, he would never leave me, that if he said jump, I would jump; if he said hop, I would hop, and I would have to do anything and everything he told me or he'd cut my face or cripple me...."

Lana admitted seeing Cheryl and telling her to go back to her bedroom, not wanting her listen to the arguing. Then, she closed the door. "I turned to Mr. Stompanato after I had closed the door, and I said, 'That's just great, my child has to hear all of that – the horrible – and I can't go through that anymore. And he kept swearing and threatening me."

Lana closed her eyes as tears formed and then began to speak again. "And if ... when it went beyond that, he would kill me and my daughter and my mother. He said no matter what, he would get me where it would hurt the most — and that would be my daughter and mother."

Fearing for their lives, Lana recounted Cheryl racing to the kitchen and returning outside her bedroom door with a nine-inch butcher knife. Lana explained what happened next to the hushed courtroom, "Everything happened so quickly – I did not even see the knife in my daughter's hand."

Lana told the court that Stompanato had a jacket and shirt hanging in the closet. "I forget exactly why it was there, or if he had brought it as a change from his apartment. Anyway, it was hanging there, and he walked away from me and went to the closet and it was on the – a hanger. And he walked back to me and was holding a jacket on the hanger as though as though he was going to strike me with it, and I said, 'Don't ever touch me again. I'm absolutely finished. This is the end. I want you to get out.' And after I said that, I was walking towards the bedroom door and he was right behind me and I opened it and my daughter came in."

"I thought it was so fast," Lana said of the actual moment of impact. "I truthfully thought she had hit him in the stomach, but the best I can remember, they came together and … they parted. I still never saw a blade."

"Did he ever make any grab at or lunge toward Cheryl after the stabbing?" she was asked.

"No."

"Did you see her hand touch his stomach?"

"Well, what I saw, I thought she had hit him in the stomach, because I could see that they were … like that," as Lana drew her hands together indicating the closeness between Johnny and Cheryl at the moment of impact.

"What had appeared to have hit the stomach?"

"Her right hand."

"Her right hand," McGinley repeated.

"Her right hand," Lana agreed.

"Is she right handed?"

"Yes," said Lana.

After recounting the stabbing, the deputy district attorney asked about the blood, or lack of blood, that night. "Was there any blood around the room or anything that you had cleaned up when you say you took the knife into the bathroom or anything like that?"

"No, sir," she answered.

"Did you have any blood on you that evening or on any of your clothes?"

"No, I did not."

"Were you wearing the same clothes after it happened as before the police arrived, were you wearing the same clothes?"

"I was wearing the same clothing," Lana said.

"Did you either call the police or request someone to call the police?"

"I don't think I telephoned the police. I know that I telephoned the emergency for the ambulance, and the resuscitator, and I telephoned Dr. Weber and Mr. Giesler, but I don't remember calling actual police."

Lana showed how he grabbed himself in the abdominal area, explaining he, "stumbled forward, turned around and fell on his back. He choked his hands on his throat. I ran to him and lifted up his sweater. I saw the blood… [and he] made a horrible noise in his throat …"

Lana said she and Cheryl tried to help Johnny, but were unsure what to do as they waited for the doctor. "And she was so frightened, and I kept trying to assure Cheryl that, 'It will be alright; I am sure it will be all right. The doctor will be here in just a minute. Granny had called him and we are not far away. And with that she burst out crying again and ran out of the room."

The courtroom gasped as Lana took a pause. "Please be quiet, gentlemen," pleaded Deputy Langhauser. Lana then continued, "I did not know that my daughter had telephoned her father, but he was the next one I saw. I don't know who let him in because only my daughter and Mr. Stompanato and I were there, as I believe I said, my maid does not live in; and I remember I was still trying to talk to and calling Mr. Stompanato. I can't think of – trying to slap his cheeks and he was still making horrible noises."

Lana said that both Cheryl and her father came into the room and looked at the horror unfolding before them. "Then, I cannot remember this – Mr. Crane – I believe took my daughter out of the room. I had again gone back to the aid of Mr. Stompanato."

"Then my mother came in," Lana testified. "I heard her calling from downstairs, and as she came in I got up and ran to her, and I said, 'Mother, please don't look. It's John.' And she said, 'What happened?'

Lana explained that Shortly after Dr. McDonald arrived he began trying to revive Johnny. The doctor then asked Lana to call another doctor – a Doctor Weber – to come assist him. He provided her the number, and she made the call.

After detailing the moments of the stabbing, Lana answered questions about the week preceding Good Friday. "… were there any fights between you and John Stompanato that Easter vacation week when Cheryl was in the house?"

"Yes," Lana responded.

"Would you tell us how many such fights occurred that she was in the house … approximately?"

"I can't. The Monday before, which was the 31st of March, my daughter had oral surgery, because she had two extra teeth by the wisdom and the dentist had to go in and cut some bone away and subsequently there were stitches."

"All we are asking you, Miss Turner, is were those fights that were going on between you and John Stompanato the week before this happened, did your daughter Cheryl ever hear or see the fights?"

"That's what I am trying to answer," said Lana. "Maybe I am not doing it correctly."

"Answer Yes or No."

"Yes. This one Monday."

The judge interrupted with, "For the record, I think you should get the date established."

"March 31," answered Lana.

"In this fight with John Stompanato, was there pretty strong language at that time?"

"Yes."

"Did your daughter ever come into the place where the argument was going on and hear any of it?"

"No, but her bedroom door was open and I had left it open because it was difficult for her to call out after the surgery, and my mother was working and Cheryl and I were alone in my mother's apartment. I kept saying to Mr. Stompanato, 'Will you keep your voice down, do not shout so loud. Her door is open and I had to leave it open in case she calls me.' – Which one time she did call and I just barely heard her say, 'Mamma, Mamma,' because her throat was so sore or mouth needed tending."

Lana continued to try to explain the circumstances behind the earlier fight until McGinley changed the course of questioning, "Did you ever talk to your daughter about the arguments you were having."

"Not until that night," Lana answered.

"What night?"

"Monday night."

Lana claimed that Johnny threatened to cut her that night, and Cheryl got a sense of the trouble her mother was in. "He went into the bathroom and he got a razor and he came and grabbed my head, all the time screaming at me violent things. Then he said that it may only start with a little one now, just give me a taste of it and even so, he would do worse. I pleaded, I said I would do anything, anything, just please don't hurt me. 'If you claim you love me, how can you hurt me? Please don't.'" Lana told the packed courtroom.

"As he let go of me, he said. 'That's just to let your know I am not kidding. Don't think you can ever get away.'"

"He cut you with a razor this time?"

"No," she answered.

When she finished her testimony, the coroner asked for a 15-minute recess, and the press immediately surrounded Lana. She looked as if she was on the verge of fainting so Jerry Giesler moved her away from crowd.

The inquest didn't end with Lana's testimony. Police later testified that they were confused by some of the details during their investigation. For starters, the knife was supposedly brand new, but it was scratched and chipped as if it had been in use for some time. In addition, there were no fingerprints on the knife. While these details seemed to have no clear explanation, there was also the fact that no blood was found on Lana's clothes or in the bedroom. But there was also little blood on the victim due to the nature of his wound and the way he landed on the floor.

Police also were puzzled at the fact that the room was in such an orderly state with such a violent altercation having gone on there. The bedroom was not in any sort of disarray, according to the authorities. And lastly, police found that the blood on the knife contained "several light and dark fibers or hairs," which could not be identified. Due to the number of people in and out of the house after the crime, it was hard to fault Lana Turner for any odd discoveries from the investigation.

As the testimony concluded, a mysterious man jumped up from the courtroom gallery, shouted that he wanted to testify. While being escorted from the courtroom, he began shouting, "Lies! All lies! This mother and daughter were both in love with Stompanato! Johnny was a gentleman!"

The man was never publicity identified, though some suspected that he worked for Mickey Cohen. The man was taken away and disappeared.

Stephen Crane with Lana and Mildred in court

SEVENTEEN

"I can't go through any more."

- Lana Turner

"Overwhelmed by the crushing strain of her ordeal, she had to be taken home before the jury of 10 men and two women brought in the unanimous verdict."

The Los Angeles Times, April 12, 1958

THE VERDICT IS IN

After her testimony, Lana was exhausted. After more than an hour on the witness stand answering questions, Lana was, "on the brink of collapse," affirmed by those in attendance said

As she stepped off the stand, the coroner asked for a short recess, and the press immediately surrounded the movie star. She was on the verge of fainting when Jerry Giesler escorted her away from the crowd.

While the inquest didn't end after Lana left the stand, the dramatic moments of testimony had. All that remained was a bit of testimony from police investigators about the scene, the knife and the lack of blood in Lana's pink bedroom. After the brief testimony, the jury left the courtroom to deliberate. Lana decided it had all been too much and wanted to go home.

The jurors for the inquest had been selected at random. In 1958, the deputy coroner was given the task of finding the jurors by touring the downtown area and asking people if they were willing and able to serve. Jurors received no pay for their service, and the coro-

Lana Turner picture on her way to court.

ner had to find a minimum of six people and no more than 15 to take part. If they agreed, they were given a summons to appear.

Inside the deliberation room, the 12 jurors discussed the facts they had learned and tried to determine what it all meant. Two of the jurors actually leaned toward recommending Cheryl face trial for what they felt was a crime, while the majority felt she had suffered enough and was acting out of fear for the safety of her mother. It took less than a half-hour for the 10 jurors to convince the holdouts to accept the majority ruling of justifiable homicide, even if the verdict weren't initially unanimous.

Returning to the courtroom, the jury told the courtroom that, "Acting out of fear for her life and for her mother's life, Cheryl Crane was justified in using deadly force to stop John Stompanato." The decision was unanimous, but it didn't have to be.

Lana had just returned home when she learned the news. "Thank God," she remarked with her lawyer by her side. She reportedly "collapsed into the arms of attorney Jerry Giesler," and had to be put to bed with sedatives.

Cheryl was not at the hearing when the decision was read. Her father, Stephen Crane, reportedly wept openly as he heard the verdict saying, "No one will ever know how grateful I am."

However, for Cheryl, she was not entirely off the hook. She had just weathered the first and most difficult hurdle. A formal court hearing would take place on April 24 and everyone wanted to know if Cheryl would be released.

Cheryl's lawyer, Arthur J. Crowley, told reporters, "Our position is that we simply wish to cooperate with the juvenile court. If they want her to remain in Juvenile Hall, we wish to cooperate to the fullest. Actually we haven't even discussed the possibility of her release. We've been too busy getting ready for this inquest matter."

In the end it didn't matter, as the court required that she

remain in juvenile detention until the court agreed with the verdict reached in the inquest. While the ruling from an inquest carries a great deal of weight with the court, it's never a guarantee that the court will automatically agree with the ruling.

After the verdict, District Attorney McKesson told the press, "After what I've heard today, and unless some new facts are uncovered, it would not be my inclination to prosecute her [Cheryl] on criminal charges."

While Cheryl remained in custody, both Lana and her father paid regular visits to her to cheer her up and assure her the end of the nightmare was near. Her father even brought boxes of candy to give out to the 19 other girls who were also being detained with her daughter at the time. Cheryl told her father that she was homesick, but no one really knew exactly what home she might have missed the most.

The Beverly Hills courthouse, 1958.

She would never return to North Bedford Drive, however, speculation as to whose custody she would be released into had the press guessing. Some feared Lana would be in for a fight against her ex-husband in attempting to obtain full custody of Cheryl. The real risk came from the Santa Monica division of the juvenile probation department when they began an investigation into Lana's personal life and its impact on her daughter. They had 10 days to complete the report as to whether Lana was fit to be a mother.

On April 24, at 2 p.m., Cheryl and her parents met in closed court in Santa Monica with Judge Allen T. Lynch to learn her fate. While speculation ranged from her being placed in a foster home to being given to her mother, father or grandmother; most agreed it was unlikely that the judge, who was a father himself, would charge Cheryl with murder.

After speaking with Cheryl at some length, Judge Lynch made his ruling. Cheryl would be placed in the care of her grandmother with once-a-week visitation rights given to both her parents. The tearful hearing ended with the decision remaining in place for 60 days, and the judge willing to consider a revision in late June. Cheryl was formally made a ward of the court.

After the inquest, Lana moved out of the home she rented on Canyon Drive, and moved Cheryl and her mother into the home. Since Lana's mother Mildred was assigned as Cheryl's guardian after the tragedy and two lawsuits were facing Lana in the aftermath of Johnny's death, Cheryl needed a stable home. The press labeled Lana a bad influence for a young girl, Lana initially moved herself into Mildred's apartment and began looking for a more permanent location. She found a home in the Roxbury Drive area of Beverly Hills, not far from the Bedford Drive home.

Roxbury Drive was home to many celebrities and offered some anonymity due to the number of stars living in the area. Names like Jimmy Stewart, Lucille Ball, Jack Benny and others called the area home. Lana found a small bungalow to lay low.

Rumors continued that Cheryl, being a minor, had lied for her mother and Lana had actually stabbed Stompanato to death. No such admission from either women would ever be made, and no evidence to that effect was ever found.

Paramount rushed *Another Time, Another Place* into theaters shortly after the trial, hoping that fans would flock to the theater to see Lana Turner's latest movie. The film didn't do well at the box office, and Lana's production company was on the hook for the less-than-stellar performance. Lana figured that the public was through with her. With the legal fees looming over her and Cheryl, she found herself in debt.

Making matters worse the Stompanato family filed a civil suit against Lana and Steve for $762,500 claiming that it was their negligence that "incited Cheryl in inflicting the fatal wound." One claim even suggested that Johnny had been stabbed by Lana while he was lying down. Their claim focused on the fact that no blood was found in the room and had he been stabbed standing up, his blood would have ended up somewhere. Lana was required to again testify in court - this time a closed one. Giesler dragged the case out until the Stompanato family settled for a mere $20,000. Later in the year, Steve Crane would appeal the court ruling making Cheryl a ward of the court, but the appeal was rejected.

While the press wasn't much on Lana's side, she did receive support from her fans. It was one of the things that helped her move on. Bob Osborne, a friend of Lana's recalled, "Lana was funny, witty, and you didn't have to know her very long to understand how she survived that scandal," he said. "Everybody liked her. She was a good egg."

She also received mountains of letters of support, even when the press was slamming her as a bad mother. So, she ultimately decided that the likely move was to get back to work. It was now time to move on – how that would happen was the million-dollar question, but the answer would soon come.

EIGHTEEN

*"Oh, Mama, stop acting. Stop trying
to shift people around as though they
were pawns on a stage."*
                    - Susie (Sandra Dee),
                        'Imitation of Life'

It would mark her first big screen appearance since the tragedy of true life unfolded. Would fans accept her? The glamorous tale would show Hollywood ... the star would not go down without a fight.

IMITATION OF LIFE

After the inquest Mickey Cohen was outraged. The coroner's verdict was a sham, according to him. If he couldn't shatter Lana through blackmail, he decided to get even another way. He went to the press. "It's the first time in my life I've ever seen a dead man convicted of his own murder," said Cohen. "So far as that jury's concerned, Johnny just walked too close to that knife."

Cohen sold the Lana Turner love letters he had stolen from Stompanato's apartment to the press, and the media had a field day with the lurid tales, splashing them across headlines and front pages for days. Even actual photos of Lana's handwritten notes were photo-copied for newspaper pages.

If there was one thing Lana Turner was accustomed to, it was being surrounded by the press and fodder for movie magazines and tabloids. There were few parts of her personal life that were off lim-its to the media, and Lana was well aware of how interested her fans were in her life. Some suggest that as her fame and popularity grew, her fans found it difficult to separate the actress from the movie star; and her life off screen became indistinguishable from the characters she played onscreen.

Her love life was perhaps the topic her fans were most inter-ested in. Being one of Hollywood's greatest beauties meant moviego-ers were interested in her romances on and off screen. Lana's leading men were often rumored to be lovers off the set, and her marriages - from the heights of romantic proposals to the lows of divorce proceedings, always made headlines. So, while the murder of her latest lover was indeed a tragic event, those who suggested her career would never recover would be sorely mistaken.

If anyone were used to picking herself up after being knocked to the ground by a whirlwind romance, it was Lana Turner. She'd rise, dust herself off, and move on to the next handsome man as well as the next glittery movie role. While it may have been a surprise to her detractors that she would recover, her fans knew it wouldn't be long before she'd be back.

While some may have expected Lana to lay low for a long while, the legal shenanigans of 1958 were as costly to her finances as they were to her movie star image. Lana needed to work. After the court proceedings, she was asked if she planned to keep working. "A great part of me would very much like not to continue," she said. "I wish I could say that I have enough [money] put away so that I wouldn't have to work. I don't. I must continue working. The fact is that it's the only thing I know and that I have been the sole support of my daughter and my mother."

Ross Hunter would present Lana with the opportunity of a lifetime when he approached her to film an update of Fannie Hurst's

Lana in a promotional shot for "Imitation of Life."

1933 novel, *Imitation of Life*, but she almost passed the opportunity by. The story was originally made for the big screen back in 1934 in a successful version starring Claudette Colbert, and Lana wasn't sure a remake of the tale had much to offer. It was the story of two single mothers - one white and one black - who work together becoming successful businesswomen. The characters also struggle with drama and emotions from raising their daughters, and Lana had concerns that this part of the story might hit a little too close to home.

Hunter was determined to make movies that he loved. He once told head of Universal, William Goetz, that he wanted to make "big, fat love stories." In fact, he first told Goetz that he wanted to remake the 30s soap-sudser, *Magnificent Obsession*, starring Rock Hudson. "I told Goetz, 'Rock is better than the westerns and tits-and-sand stuff he's been in. Clean him up and you're going to have a great, big, smashing romantic star on your hands.' Goetz said, 'No one wants to see this kind of movie anymore, but I'll give you $850,000 to make it.'"

Hunter was able get Jane Wyman as his leading lady, and the movie was a huge hit. Hunter and Hudson would go on to become close friends and make another five movies together. For his next picture, it wasn't the male lead he was focused on. It was his leading lady, Lana Turner.

The executives at Universal called Hunter mad for wanting to cast Lana Turner in the lead of his next film. "That's exactly why I wanted her," recalled Hunter. "It was two months after the killing, and everyone else in town considered her finished - an untouchable. At first, she turned down the script, because she thought it was too close to her own life, her own daughter. But every woman in the world said, 'Oooh, if I could only be Lana for one minute.' Every woman would like to have a stud like Johnny Stompanato – dead or alive, Lana had him."

Hunter was used to the dismay of Hollywood executives.

"Universal wouldn't give me money to buy great scripts, so I had to depend on a look, an image," he once said. "Universal thought I was crazy," he added, "but I believed that an industry that produced two or three hundred movies a year had to make four or five pictures about the beautiful people."

Hunter continued asking Lana, but she still said no. "I can't do it. The theme is too close to home," she said. But Hunter refused to take no for an answer and sent her dozens of roses to get her to meet with him about the script. She finally agreed, and the two met on the beach in Malibu, and as they strolled along the sand, he read her the script aloud. "She cried through most of it," Hunter claimed, but she was still reluctant.

Hunter persisted, explaining that he wanted to update the story by making Lana's character a successful actress and that the modern day exploration of racism would set the story apart from any real life tales from Lana's recent past. What sold Lana was the fact that it would be a glossy and glamorous soap opera, directed by Douglas Sirk. And to top it off, she would be dressed in gowns by Jean Louis and jewels from Laykin et Cie. On the downside, Lana was only offered a small salary for the part, because the studio saw her as a risky choice. However, in exchange, Hunter was able to offer her half the net box office if the film were a hit.

Another plus for Lana was a chance to star opposite handsome leading man John Gavin. Hunter had an eye for pairing the two and felt the casting would draw an audience in. "I can predict whether two actors are going to spark. Chemistry enhances glamour. Period," said Hunter.

Lana was still concerned about how it would look to movie audiences, so soon after the tragedy. "You'll have to face life sometime, dear," Hunter told her. "It's a great role, and I think people will admire you for doing it."

While Lana was clearly the star of the picture, she accepted the part for a mere $2,500 a week knowing it was a gamble for her, Hunter and Universal. The supporting cast included Juanita Moore, Dan O'Herlihy, and Susan Kohner. Mahalia Jackson was also added to the cast for a notable funeral sequence in which she sings "Trouble of the World." In the role of Lana's daughter, Hunter cast Sandra Dee, whom he saw as a squeaky clean teenager - perfect for his films. "I wouldn't let her out of the house unless her hair was done and her makeup wonderful," he said of Dee. Lana would be featured with what would be called the most expensive wardrobe in movie history at the time, with reports setting her clothes and jewels in excess of $1.078 million.

In the updated version, Lana plays Lora Meredith, who dreams of becoming a famous Broadway actress when the film begins in 1947. After losing track of Susie, her young daughter at the beach, she meets Steve Archer, played by John Gavin, who helps find the girl. Susie is playing with the daughter of Annie Johnson, played by Juanita Moore, a black divorcee with a daughter named Sarah Jane. Sarah Jane is of mixed-race and can pass for white, which becomes a key plot line as the story proceeds. Lora takes Annie and her daughter in and soon the four are living together with Annie taking care of the home and children while Lora pursues her acting career. Steve becomes a frequent visitor and family friend.

As the children grow older conflicts between Sarah Jane and her mother emerge as she struggles with racism and uses her mixed-race to pass for white, distancing herself from her mother. As years go by, Lora becomes a highly regarded Broadway star with Annie serving as her housekeeper and friend. More struggles with career, health and raising teenage daughters are paired with the weightier subjects of discrimination and racism. As the film concludes, Annie passes away and is given a lavish funeral, much of which she planned herself. As the final procession begins, Sarah Jane pushes through the crowd of mourners and throws herself on her mother's casket, begging for forgiveness for having abandoned her. Lora takes Sarah Jane to their waiting black limousine and along with, Susie and Steve they take Annie's casket to its final resting place.

Imitation of Life began filming August 1958, roughly four months after the scandal and wrapped in October of the same year. Lana loved being given the lush treatment by Douglas Sirk and especially loved the gowns provided by Jean Louis. According to press material, Louis would provide Lana with 34 different outfits for the picture, but some critics suggested that by their count it was more like 29. Deleted scenes account for the discrepancy. As part of the story, Lana's first look is a mere off-the-rack dress, but as the story progresses and her character becomes more and more successful, her outfits become equally more glamorous. Ross Hunter felt that it was a coup for the movie to have Louis dress Lana. "Jean is as good at creating an apron as a ball gown," he said.

Accompanying the Louis gowns, a reported $1 million worth of jewelry was provided by Laykin et Cie with armed guards hired to watch over them during production. Even while on set, guards were stationed just off camera as Lana filmed, making sure no one walked off with any of the gems. In fact, before the film actually started, Laykin et Cie had sold many of the baubles from their shop in I. Magnin, and patrons were asked for permission to allow the studio to borrow the jewels for the filming. Most agreed, and the jewels were taken by armed guards to the studio when they were needed for a specific scene. Some of the owners reportedly called the set from time to time asking, "Are my jewels working today?"

For Lana, the film was both a blessing and a curse. She needed the work. The income from the film and her name on the marquee would go a long way to help her recover from her recent tragedy. However, the story cut too close to home at times and would bring up difficult memories that the star was trying to put behind her.

Lana became very fond of Juanita Moore during the film - so much so, that one writer suggested that the actresses began to see their characters and themselves as one in the same. The two women grew close while working on the film, and Juanita recalled Lana being under great pressure and "still distraught from the Stompanato ordeal four months earlier."

Lana would occasionally whisper, "Juanita, I need to talk," and the two women would leave the set as Lana confided in Moore about her troubles off the set with lawsuits, Cheryl and the press. Lana once said, "Juanita, I was on my ass when this picture came along." And Moore responded, "Honey, you can't get any lower than that."

One of the most difficult scenes Lana encountered was towards the end of the picture during the funeral procession. "I most dreaded the part when Annie's repentant daughter would throw herself on the casket," suggesting it reminded her of her own difficult relationship with her daughter. While rehearsing the scenes in the church, Lana would recall, "I simply broke down. Images of my own life, my own dark fears flooded my mind, and I dissolved in tears. I fled."

Lana ran to her trailer where she "slumped onto the chair in front of my little dressing table, burying my face in my arms. By now I was shaking with sobs unable to control myself."

Lana's hairdresser, Patti Westmore saw her leave the set and followed her out to her dressing room trailer. Lana waved her off, trying to get her to leave, but Westmore refused. She grasped her by the shoulders, saying, "Stop it! You've got to come back and finish the scene," Lana could not stop crying, so Westmore reportedly slapped her, shocking Lana. She then put her arms around her and helped her get herself under control. Lana then returned and completed the scene.

Universal predicted the film would fail, if not everywhere,

certainly in the South. Hunter recalled "going to theaters all over the South for two months - some of them 'For Blacks Only' - telling people, 'It's not the story of a white mother and black mother, but the story of two mothers, one of whom happens to be black. I'm going to do everything I can to make a movie that will give you people a chance to go into a darkened theater and cry unashamedly.' "

When the movie finally opened, it was a smash. To promote the film, Hunter convinced Lana to take part in a cross-country tour

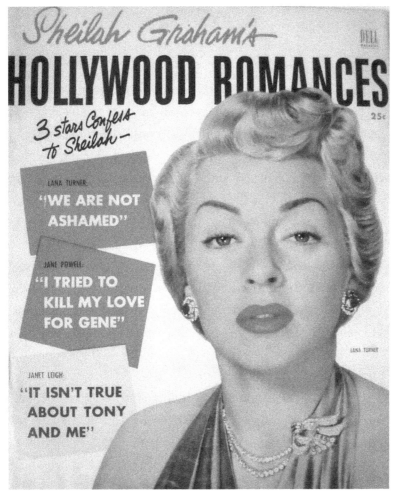

A popular cover girl before and after Johnny Stompanato.

to promote the film, which was a fairly uncommon thing to do at the time and certainly uncommon for a producer. However, Hunter saw the value. "I'd go out on tour and meet my audiences, listen to the kinds of movies they said they wanted. Whoever heard of a producer going out on the road to sell a movie right after he finishes it? Taking not necessarily the star, but the star's wardrobe, on tour? Or giving big premiere parties, lots of which I paid for? But a producer has to have a handshake with the public, to find out what will tear them away from their homes. I went out there creating an image for myself through my movies, saying, 'You're going to see a picture with real stars looking glamorous in beautiful gowns on beautiful sets. No kitchen sinks. No violence. No pores. No messages.' And it worked."

One move that helped boost the success of the film was the studio's decision to release it simultaneously to white and black movie theaters in the U.S. South. At the time, Hollywood didn't release films in black theatres until after their run in major cities and traditional white theaters. A study of audience members in 1960 revealed that 30 percent of the movie audience at the time was African-American.

The feature became Universal's top-grossing film to date and would remain there for another decade. It was also Lana's most success-ful film ever. Her deal for half the profits turned out to be the best pos-sible outcome. Made for roughly $2 million, *Imitation of Life* grossed $6.4 million in its initial U.S. release, placing number five on the year's list of top box-office films. By 1970, it had earned more than $25 million worldwide. Lana reportedly would pull in as much as $11 million during the years after the film's release.

Financially she would remain comfortable for the rest of her life. But more than that, it was her face, her career and her stardom that mattered. Her fans had not deserted her. Though it was not all roses for Lana. "As we got off the train in Chicago, Lana was shot at," recalled producer Ross Hunter. The producer was never sure "if it was by a mem-ber of the Stompanato family or a gun-happy fan," but he said, "Being the trouper that she was, Lana still got up on those stages to be interviewed before each and every showing of the movie."

It was during the filming of *Imitation of Life* that Lana also began to slowly get back into the social scene. While she wasn't about to show up at Hollywood movie premieres and major social events, she did accept an invitation to an occasional small party. At one small dinner party that summer, she met a man by the name of Fred May. May, a real estate businessman, was in the throws of a messy divorce when he was first introduced to Lana. He was reportedly shy about asking her out on a date, but Lana warmed up to him quickly. Aside from the fact that he had the handsome good looks of Tyrone Power, May also had a ranch where he raised thoroughbred horses, and Lana had long been a fan of horses and horse racing.

May asked for Lana's phone number and called her a few days later inviting her to his ranch. The two quickly hit it off and began seeing each other regularly.

NINETEEN

"They touched...and an evil spark was struck!"

- Portrait in Black, 1960

Lana sticks with the tried and true soap opera drama for the glamorous story of a woman with murder on her mind, but would her fans see shades of real life on the screen?

PORTRAIT IN BLACK

Premiering in New York on April 17, 1959, *Imitation of Life* was released nationwide on April 30 and immediately found its audience. Budgeted at $2 million, the film became a huge success for Universal, as well as for Lana. Since Ross Hunter was able to keep costs down by getting Turner's gowns and jewels on loan, the film looked far more costly than it really was. Douglas Sirk's lush direction and cinematography put Lana in her best light, making the film the glossy tearjerker fans were hoping for. It earned nearly $6.5 million in its domestic release and continued to pull in strong box office during its international release, with some reports putting the film's take at the $25 million mark. Lana's cut of the proceeds put her on sound financial footing after the legal fiasco surrounding the death of Johnny Stompanato. The success of the film showed her fans had not deserted her.

While reviewers felt the film was nothing more than a glossy soap opera and brushed the film off, fans flocked to see Lana Turner as the mother of a troubled teenage daughter, making the film Univer-

Lana and Anthony Quinn on the set of "Portrait in Black."

sal's biggest hit to date. It would remain in that top spot for more than a decade until another Ross Hunter picture, *Airport*, broke that record in 1970. For Lana, it was just the shot her career needed. Fans ate it up, putting Lana was back on top at the box office with the film becoming her biggest financial success. It would enable Lana to remain comfortable for the rest of her life, even if she didn't make another movie.

If *Imitation of Life's* success owed anything to the story's similarities to Lana's private life, her next picture would cut even closer to home. Upon the heels of *Imitation of Life*, Ross Hunter and Universal were eager to work with Lana on a follow-up picture. And Lana, knowing she could earn a hefty profit and be adorned with gowns and jewels on the big screen for her fans, was more than willing to participate.

The project they chose was *Portrait in Black*. The story was based on a play that had premiered in London in 1946 and on Broadway a year later. The play had starred Diana Wynyard, and whose husband, Carol Reed, planned to direct Universal's film version. Screen rights to the stage production were purchased soon after the show's premiere, but it was originally planned as a vehicle for Joan Crawford as the star. When Reed backed out due to disagreements with Universal over the screen adaptation of the story, the screenplay began gathering dust. In June 1950, Universal sold the rights back to the play's writers, and Michael Gordon and Joan Crawford were reportedly again interested in bringing it to the screen. No film surfaced though, and the story lay dormant again until it resurfaced in 1954 when reports that brothers Edmond and Liam O'Brien were hoping to adapt the play into a film that would be shot in Italy. No stars were mentioned and the idea again was never realized.

The screenplay languished until Hunter dusted it off as another glossy, suspenseful soap opera for Lana. In October 1959, *The*

Hollywood Reporter mentioned that Lawrence Harvey would co-star in a version of the film, but other reports suggested a variety of leading male stars opposite Lana, including Louis Jourdan, Van Johnson, Richard Burton and Peter Finch in the role of Lana's lover, Dr. David Rivera.

Originally Lana planned on another film project before moving onto *Portrait in Black*, so the Hunter picture would have to wait. In early 1959, she signed on to make *Anatomy of a Murder* for direc-

Lana in a publicity shot for "Portrait in Black."

tor Otto Preminger. Lana had been Preminger's first choice for the key role of Laura in the film. In fact, Lana actually had started working on the film in the first months of the year, but exited the feature in late February. There was some discrepancy as to whether she left the role or was fired. Lee Remick, who replaced Lana in film, recalled that she had been told by her agent that Preminger had fired Lana, but Preminger said Turner had quit the film when he announced Remick as her replacement to the press on March 4. Lana said she made the decision to remove herself from the picture after calling her agent and telling him, "Get me out of this film."

The disagreement over the part came over wardrobe, a topic about which Lana felt obviously very strongly after her lustrous treatment on *Imitation of Life*. She knew how to be dressed to look her best, and Lana had definite ideas about her clothes. Lana recalled that preparations for the film were "moving along nicely until costuming time, when Hope Bryce, Preminger's assistant, wanted to dress me in a simple little suit right off the racks. I have never favored ready-to-wear clothing onscreen. So I suggested my dressmaker run up the kind of suit she had in mind."

Lana wrote in her autobiography that Preminger called her that evening shouting at her over the suggestion. Preminger remembered the incident differently, saying Lana complained that her clothes were "not glamorous enough." He recalled telling her that he was "trying to achieve a certain kind of realism, that I was not interested in old-fashioned glamour."

Lana left the production, disappointing Preminger over the loss. "With Miss Turner, I would have played the part differently. It would have been a study of the lieutenant's fascination with an older woman, and she would have been excellent in it."

Imitation of Life would hit theaters that April and find fantastic business at the box office, allowing Lana to take some time before jumping onto her next project after *Anatomy of a Murder* fell through. Still, Lana was at the studio signing contracts for the next Universal film, not long after *Imitation of Life* started raking in profits. She would step onto the soundstages to begin production on December 14, 1959, and even with a short break for Christmas and New Year's, she was back at work and able to complete the film by late January 1960.

Lana got another career boost when she learned that she had received a star on the Hollywood Walk of Fame that year. Located at 6241 Hollywood Boulevard, her star was assigned on February 8, 1960, but the new walk was in fact still in development. Construction actually began on February 8 for the long-planned Walk, which had been in the works since about 1953. While eight stars were laid back in 1958 as a demonstration of what the walk would ultimately look like, the first star to be laid in the actual Walk was that of Stanley Kramer on March 28, 1960. The additional selection of the initial stars to be featured, including Lana's, were set to be laid during the later months until the dedication ceremony on November 23, 1960, as a highlight of the Hollywood Christmas Parade. Lana was delighted to be one of the first stars selected for the honor.

Portrait in Black was a suspense thriller that had Lana suffering at the hands of a controlling husband dying of cancer, played by Lloyd Nolan. He runs a major shipping line in San Francisco and is under the care of a doctor, who is having an affair with his wife, played by Lana. Anthony Quinn was hired on to the key role of Dr. Rivera and the two lovers conspire to kill her husband, but soon after they find that someone knows their secret. Lana's character begins receiving threatening letters from someone who knows what they've done. They suspect everyone, including the housekeeper, chauffeur, her husband's business partner and her stepdaughter. The plot thickens as more murder plots are revealed, and nobody seems to know whom to trust.

Lana was once again dressed to the nines, covered in glittering jewels to the tune of a reported $1,175,000 and placed in luxurious settings. Filmed in part on location in San Francisco, the grand house used in the film, at Broadway and Baker Streets, was owned by friends of Ross Hunter's. Many interiors were filmed on

Lana during a costume test for "Portrait in Black."

Universal soundstages in Hollywood, however, a number of notable locations included the Pacific Coast Highway and Devil's Slide; as well as the I. Magnin Department Store in San Francisco's Union Square; Golden Gate Park's Japanese Tea House; an apartment on Divisadero Street, where the adulterous love affair with her husband's doctor takes place; and several piers along San Francisco's historic waterfront.

Universal held the world premiere for the film in Chicago on June 23, 1960. A number of the stars, including Lana, Anthony Quinn and Sandra Dee helped promote the film by touring the country for other premieres in New York and Los Angeles. While the film didn't pull in as much as *Imitation of Life*, it earned a respectable $3.6 million, which made it a profitable film for Universal, considering Ross Hunter was able to keep the cost of the expensive looking movie relatively low. Lana would come out with a nice profit for the film as well with her cut of the proceeds.

In addition to the standard movie campaign, to promote the film, Universal negotiated tie-ins with several fashion, photography and publishing companies, focusing on Lana's jewels, hair and costumes. Bantam Books published a "pocket edition" of the story for booksellers.

For Lana, it was still too good to be true. She had weathered the 1950s only to come out on top in 1960 with a strong career and a rebounding personal life. She took another shot at marriage in November 1960 when she wed rancher Fred May - a member of the family that owned the May Co. department store chain. The two reportedly had great chemistry, and Lana loved that he came from outside her usual Hollywood set. However, her fifth marriage didn't last and the couple would divorce in October 1962.

Lana also had her challenges with Cheryl. While living with her mother, Cheryl began to rebel from her three guardians. While her mother and father angled for her time, Cheryl spent the bulk of her time with her grandmother, Mildred. At her age, Mildred wasn't prepared to deal with a troubled teenager. Mildred was known to enjoy her cocktails in the evening and to retire early to bed, leaving Cheryl the opportunity to sneak out of the house. She had been dating a boy in 1960 and would spend the evening with him. The two decided to elope, until Lana and Stephen Crane caught wind of the plans. Instead of ordering her to abandon the relationship, mother and father decided to take a new tact and supported the idea, suggesting the pair have a big church wedding. Cheryl backed off.

However, one evening Cheryl was picked up by the police and found she had violated her probation and curfew and was sentenced to a reform school in the San Fernando Valley called El Retiro. Hating the place, Cheryl ran away twice. Her troubles would continue for several more years until she became an adult and had the chance to make her own decisions.

At a party around the time of premiere of *Portrait in Black,* Fred May ended up in a shouting match and near fist-fight with *Hollywood Reporter* columnist Mike Connolly, after he had overheard Connolly disparaging Lana and Cheryl to another guest. May grabbed the columnist by the tie and said, "I love this girl and what you're writing about her is unfair." Insults ensued and Lana ended up in tears; but was grateful for May's standing up for her.

The film might have done better at the box office, but Alfred Hitchcock's *Psycho* was luring in all the suspense moviegoers in the summer of 1960. The Hitchcock film was a huge box office hit, earning more than $9 million in its initial release that year - and on a budget of only about $860,000. Released about 10 days earlier than *Portrait in Black*, it earned much of the attention at the box office that summer. A number of other notable box office hits outshined Lana's film that year, including *Spartacus, Exodus, Butterfield 8, Oceans 11,* and *The Apartment.*

TWENTY

*"ALL OF THEM WERE BY LOVE
POSSESSED! The bold best-seller
that sent a fever through America
now fires the screen!"*
                    - By Love Possessed, 1961

After the success of 'Imitation of Life' and assignment to
'Portrait in Black' Lana had shown not only that she was
capable of completing a film, but also that the public would
turn
out to watch it.

By LOVE
POSSESSED

Between 1959 and 1961 Lana had a handful of other projects
come her way that she considered doing. She might have done any
one of them had the script or the money been right. For Lana, fortunately, she could afford to be choosy with her finances in such good
shape.

Streets of Montmartre was proposed as a likely follow-up

to *Imitation of Life* and would have been ideal for Lana. Based on a novel by Stephen and Ethel Longstreet, Douglas Sirk had planned to direct the film about the life of Suzanne Valadon, a successful model who was best known as a companion to renowned painters Toulouse-Lautrec, Renoir, and Degas. Lana would have been set in the best of lighting, costumes, jewelry, and would have starred opposite the handsome Louis Jourdan. The feature was set to be filmed in Paris, and Lana would certainly have been intrigued by the glamorous picture considering Sirk would have shot her at her best. However, Sirk fell into ill health after completing *Imitation of Life,* and the film was delayed indefinitely. Sirk ultimately would retire to Switzerland and the picture would never be made, with or without Lana.

Luanne Royal was another picture Lana turned down around the same period. A planned Ross Hunter production, the story was written by George Zuckerman, author of *Written on the Wind*, another Douglas Sirk film. Lana reportedly didn't like the script, which was described as a "turbulent, exciting, love story about a woman who falls in love with her doctor."

Two other films, *The Colonel's Lady* and *The Chalk Garden* were also offered to Lana in the 1960-61 time frame. The first was an original story planned by Universal that never saw the light of day, while the second was based on a successful Broadway play. Ross Hunter would produce the film with Lana as its star. Hunter initially thought an English setting would be too dreary and planned to set Lana in Carmel, California for the film, but Lana opted out and Deborah Kerr would take her place. Hunter would ultimately drop the Carmel concept and stick more closely to the original story.

One script Lana did sign on for was *By Love Possessed*. A United Artists release, produced by Seven Arts and Mirisch Pictures, the film was based on a hugely successful 1957 novel, but had a dreadful time getting to the big screen.

The screenplay for the film was reportedly penned by writer John Dennis; however, Dennis was actually a pseudonym because the original writer refused to be associated with the script. Charles Schnee was an Academy-Award winning writer who walked away with an Oscar for *The Bad and the Beautiful*, another Lana Turner

Lana rebounded after the drama of 1958 with several hit movies and a new lease on life and love.

picture from 1953. Schnee had the difficult task of taking a 575-page novel that tries to chronicle a 25-year period and condensing it to a tale that takes place over the course of about a month. It focused on what love can do to people, or cause people to do because of it. After he delivered his draft of the script, the producers brought in three other writers, Isobel Lennar, Bill Roberts and Ketti Frings to help refine the script before production began.

While the novel's author, James Gould Cozzens, would win the William Dean Howells Award for the "most distinguished work of American fiction published in the last five years." Schnee needed to jettison much of the story to center on a brief present three-day period, to cut the story down for acceptable film.

After the script was completed, Schnee saw the finished version and hit the roof. He threatened to sue the producers if his name wasn't taken off the screenplay; so, they created the pseudonym to avoid legal issues.

Directed by John Sturges, Lana Turner was given star billing and paid $300,000 to star, but she held considerably less screen time than her costars, Jason Robards, George Hamilton and Efrem Zimbalist, Jr. The producers hoped that the film would capture the same interest as *Peyton Place* had several years earlier and even set the story in New England like *Peyton Place* instead of the original book's location of Pennsylvania. The promotion of the picture also aimed to capture a similar look as the earlier film, and a theme song from Vic Damone, offered a glossy feel of *Imitation of Life*.

It was Sturges' first film after the success of *The Magnificent Seven* and he filmed the story quickly over a period of about 32 days. Though shot mostly on soundstages of Hollywood, the film had some location shooting taking place in Groton and Fitchburg Massachusetts to capture scenic backgrounds in color by DeLuxe. DeLuxe color was an Eastmancolor-based process for improved color compositing, similar to Technicolor. It was hoped it might add that extra bit of luster to the feature.

For Lana, again the challenge was trying to balance the need to look the part of a housewife, but still to bring glamour to the big screen. Since her character was wealthy, she was able to ensure the proper use of gowns and fashion-forward dresses making her look her best. Bill Thomas, one of the costume designers from *Imitation of Life*, was hired to dress Lana for her role in the film. "Lana was the most clothes-conscious star I ever worked with," he said. "She knew fabric and color, and what worked for her, like nobody I ever met."

The story centers on three partners of a Massachusetts law firm, Arthur Winner, Julius Penrose and Noah Tuttle. Their personal lives and careers are intertwined in a story that weaves legal woes and marital infidelity and includes a host of plot points like car crashes, love affairs, rape, embezzlement and suicide.

Lana plays Marjorie Penrose, the wife of one law partner and the mistress of another. Marjorie is unsatisfied with her marriage because her husband, Julius, played by Jason Robards, has been impotent since a car crash. Deep down she wants to find a way to make the marriage work, but her drinking and behavior get in the way. At the same time Arthur Winner, played by Efrem Zimbalist Jr., begins to suspect a senior partner in his firm is stealing money, and a lull in his marriage leads him to a dangerous liaison with Marjorie. Meanwhile Arthur's son, played by George Hamilton, gets caught up in a rape charge and the characters meander through a maze of discontent as the story lurches to its end. Other notable supporting cast included Susan Kohner, Thomas Mitchell, Everett Sloane, Carroll O'Connor and Barbara Bel Geddes.

It was during the period of filming and release of *By Love Possessed* that Lana married Fred May. Married at the Miramar Hotel in Santa Monica on November 27, 1960, it was just one day before their marriage license expired, having been taken out earlier in the year. Lana gushed, "He's such a wonderful guy. I wish I'd met him years earlier."

As for the film, it was released in July 1961 and reviewers instantly made the comparisons to *Peyton Place*. The producers had actually hoped to recapture the success of Lana's earlier film, but many felt the move was "a talky affair," and lacked the drama and action of the earlier film and the luster of a Douglas Sirk feature. *The New Yorker* tried to be kind to the film, with Brendan Gill writing, "Almost everyone concerned with *By Love Possessed* appears to have been honorably determined to do his best," but he felt that the producers were struggling with "a work that contained few traces of filmable material."

All was not lost however when Inflight Motion Pictures came up with a process for delivering a 16mm film service on commercial aircraft in 1961. This advancement resulted in the first feature film title being shown to first-class passengers on a regular commercial airline flight on Trans World Airlines. *By Love Possessed* made history as that first feature film.

TWENTY ONE

"Humor has been the balm of my life, but it's been reserved for those close to me, not part of the public Lana."

- Lana Turner

*After touring with Bob Hope to entertain the troops, Lana
agrees to take to the big screen with the comedy legend,
looking for a hit and a change of pace from the drama on
and off the screen.*

BACHELOR IN PARADISE

Some critics suggested that Bob Hope was in a cinematic
decline in 1961 when he starred in *Bachelor in Paradise*. At nearly
58 years old, Hope had weathered the entertainment industry's ups
and downs for decades. His comedic talents had been tested on the
live circuit, radio, TV and film. Most recently known for his live
tours to boost morale of the armed services, Hope found touring a
gratifying effort that made him one of the most popular and endearing

comedians of the twentieth century. His touring often brought a host of celebrities along for the ride and both actors, comedians, musicians and a host of beauties traveled with him. Lana Turner had been one of those women. The two were friendly, and Hope had one day hoped to co-star with her in a feature film.

Nearing 60, Bob Hope was no longer the youthful comedian he had been in his prime. While still riding high, his solo feature films had not been as successful as his comedies with co-star Bing Crosby. The team's 'Road" pictures had witty banter and comedic plot lines that outshined many of his later efforts. And Hope had a counter-balance to his witty sarcasm. These days, aside from his military performances, Hope was best known as the host of the annual Academy Awards ceremonies.

Lana, on the other hand, was just 40 and had fared better in recent screen efforts. *Bachelor in Paradise* was a chance for her to

Lana tried her hand at comedy in 1961, alongside Bob Hope, in "Bachelor in Paradise."

take a different role and present another side of her acting efforts – comedy. Directed by Jack Arnold, the film would help take Hope in a new direction as well. While the film was far from a major hit, it did earn some good reviews.

For Lana, *Bachelor in Paradise* meant a return to MGM after a five-year absence. While successful with glossy soap operas and dramas, Lana faced less proven ground with comedy. But the return to MGM also gave her a chance to work with old friends like cinematographer Joseph Ruttenberg and costume designer Helen Rose.

Another major factor in her agreeing to do the film was financial. After leaving MGM in 1956, Lana reportedly signed an agreement to film one movie a year over a five-year period at minimal salary in exchange for a full pension from the studio. *Bachelor in Paradise* would actually be the only film made under the terms of the contract. While Lana wouldn't benefit from the full pension she hoped for when she signed the deal, the film would net her roughly $92,000 from the studio pension fund.

Bachelor in Paradise also offered Lana a chance to continue working. Even if the money weren't the goal, the fame was part of what kept her going and gave her purpose to put the personal dramas of the last few years behind her. Problems with Cheryl at home continued. Around the time of filming, Cheryl agreed to a voluntary stay at the Institute of Living for Psychiatric Treatment in Hartford, Connecticut in an effort to sort out her problems away from her mother. Filming *Bachelor in Paradise* was a welcome escape to a lighthearted comedy.

In the film, Hope plays A.J. Niles, a provocative, best-selling author who finds himself in a jam after discovering he owes a large tax debt to the IRS after being swindled by his accountant. He's convinced to go undercover using an alias, "Jack Adams," and to move into a California suburban community called Paradise Village to research a new book about the sex lives of middle-class America.

Niles is pursued by a flirtatious married woman but falls for Lana's character, Rosemary, instead. Lana is the real estate agent who rents her home to him as a place for him to do his research. The two become entangled in comedic moments as he fakes his way through the story, and she gradually falls for him while doing everything she can to fight him off. While in divorce court, after being accused of ruining a number of the marriages of his neighbors in the small community, Niles reveals his love for Rosemary and asks her to marry him.

Much of the filming took place on location in a real suburban community and used actual locations for a number of significant scenes, adding authenticity to the film. Hope's character visits a shopping center where eggs are on sale for 42 cents a dozen, as well as a bowling alley and a drive-thru hamburger stand. Lana even appears in an actual Pig Pit barbecue restaurant, where her character does the hula while a bit intoxicated, and Hope's character watches delightfully.

Lana and Bob Hope in a scene from "Bachelor in Paradise."

The boom of suburbia was nearly as much of a character in the film as the actors. The cinematic shots display the variety styles of new neighborhoods and housing that were cropping up across America. The distances between home and work meant an increase in the commuter distance and the expanding highway system were often on

display in the film. The producers apparently made a deal with Chrysler for filming with a wide variety of the car company's latest models heavily featured in the film. Hope, who had a longtime deal with Buick as a spokesperson, would end that relationship around the time of the feature, which some have called "a 90-minute commercial for Chrysler products."

The climax of the film takes place in court with Agnes Moorehead in a cameo as the court judge. Also co-starring in the film was Jim Hutton. Hutton was relatively new to the Hollywood scene. *Bachelor in Paradise* was his second time working with Paula Prentiss, who was also relatively new to the business. The young actors first worked together in 1960's *Where the Boys Are*.

Bob Hope, saw the film as a more adult comedy similar to his previous film, *The Facts of Life*, co-starring Lucille Ball. During *Bachelor in Paradise,* Hope was still recovering from eye surgery. The adult comedy appealed to him; since it focused more on dialogue for the laughs and less on slapstick comedy, which helped him avoid more physical stunts required in some of his other film projects.

Bachelor in Paradise was released in 1961 in Metrocolor, MGM's trade name for films processed at their laboratory using Kodak's Eastmancolor film. The comedy used the tagline "He's the world's greatest authority on love... and she has a few ideas of her own!" MGM records reported the film took in $2.5 million at the box office in the United States and Canada and another $1 million during its worldwide release. And while the returns were far from shabby, reports say the cost of the picture left it losing some $344,000.

A.H. Weiler of *The New York Times* reviewed the film, writing, "If Bob Hope seems less spirited than the gay blade who dashed down all those "Road" comedies and more a mature gent toting a bag full of quips up a hill in "Bachelor in Paradise," the trek seems worthwhile. For his latest caper, which was unveiled at the Capitol yesterday, has enough sharp gags to make his recent TV spectaculars unspectacular even though the romantic antics on which it is all pegged are somewhat less than inspired. This pleasantly varicolored "Paradise" may not be heavenly but its mild fun and frolics should keep a viewer reasonably happy."

As for Lana's performance, the reviewer noted, "Lana Turner, as the efficient charmer who keeps Hope springing eternally, does not set new acting standards but is certain to make the ladies dis-

Bob Hope and Lana Turner in a scene from the film.

contented. Her wardrobe—there appears to be a new change in every scene—is resplendent enough to drive the haute couture echelon to distraction."

The film, however, did earn three Laurel awards - one for Best Comedy, another for Best Comedy Actor for Bob Hope and a third for Best Song "Bachelor in Paradise." Hope was also nominated for the Golden Globe Award for Best Actor – Motion Picture Musical or Comedy.

Ironically enough, it wasn't actually Lana or Hope that got the biggest career boost from *Bachelor in Paradise*. The title song by Henry Mancini and Mack David won an Oscar nomination after the film's release and during the Academy Awards, Ann-Margret was invited to perform the tune on live television. Little known to audiences Ann-Margret's only role to date had been as Bette Davis's estranged daughter in 1961's *Pocketful of Miracles*. Her Oscar performance helped make her a star, and she'd follow it up with a starring role in the film version of the musical *Bye Bye Birdie*.

TWENTY TWO

"A successful man is one who makes more money than his wife can spend. A successful woman is one who can find such a man."

- Lana Turner

The movie star returns to the world of comedy again, this time with Dean Martin as her husband in a humorous tale of a wife trying to stop her husband's addiction to gambling.

WHO'S GOT THE ACTION?

Lana had always had a thing for Dean Martin. Tall, dark and handsome, Dean shared many of the same physical attributes that Johnny Stompanato had. There was nothing she enjoyed more than being on the arm of a man like that – or in their bed.

In fact, in the late 1940s, Lana and Dean traveled in the same social circle. Ciro's was a popular hangout for the young Hollywood set, and both Lana and Dean were known to frequent the locale. One of the men who saw first hand was Herman Hover, Ciro's owner.

Located on Sunset Boulevard on the Sunset Strip, Ciro's opened in 1940 under the ownership of William Wilkerson, but Hover took over the hot spot in 1942 and ran it as the hottest club in West Hollywood until it closed its doors in 1957. Ironically enough, Hover's home at 606 North Bedford Drive was just a block away from Lana's rented home where the death of Johnny Stompanato took place in 1958.

"Ciro's did terrific," Hover said. "Everyone thought Howard Hughes was backing me, but there were no partners."

Hover said back in the early days after the club closed each night, there was always a handful of celebrities and their pals on hand. People like Howard Hughes, Frank Sinatra, Ann Sheridan and even LA mobster Mickey Cohen were frequent guests who stayed past closing. At closing time, Hover often found himself inviting his remaining guests back to his mansion, a home once owned by Alfred Vanderbilt and Mary Pickford. Both Dean and Lana had been part of the circle.

"Lana was crazy about him," recalled Hover. "In those days there was a twelve-o'clock liquor curfew. So, frequently, when the joint closed, we'd go to somebody's house, mostly mine, but sometimes, like Lana would say, 'Let's all go to my house.' There'd be about four or six of us, go up to her house, sometimes we'd bring a piano player with us, have an informal party. We really enjoyed it."

"I'd have parties almost every night at my house in Beverly Hills," said Hover. "And Lana was really stuck on him [Dean]. I saw her pull some raw stuff with Dean, with her own husband, Bob Topping, right there. She went pretty far."

But Hover never saw Dean fall for Lana's advances, and it was in his North Bedford Drive mansion, in September 1949 that Dean married Jeanne Biegger.

Flash forward to 1962 - Dean was still married to Jeanne, and

Lana was finishing up marriage number five to Fred May - when the two came together to film their only movie together, *Who's Got the Action?*

Based on the 1960 novel *Four Horse Players Are Missing* by Alexander Rose, *Who's Got the Action?* gave Lana a chance to play for laughs in a comedy film as the wife of a man with a gambling addiction. With Dean Martin as her husband, Lana enlists the help of her husband's business partner to help cure him of his addiction before he gets in too deep with his syndicate bookie, played by Walter Matthau. Produced by Jack Rose, and directed by Daniel Mann, the

Lana next joined Dean Martin for "Who's Got the Action."

movie was co-produced through Dean's own production company, Claude Productions, giving Dean a large cut of the profits, along with Paramount Pictures, the other producer of the film.

The story centers on the gambling habit of lawyer Steve Flood, played by Dean, and the troubles it causes his marriage to Melanie, played by Lana. She initially suspects him of marital infidelity and is relieved to find it's only gambling. She and Steve's law partner Clint Morgan, played by Eddie Albert, set her up as a fictitious bookie giving great terms to customers. They lure Flood into booking his bets through her with the plan for him to lose enough money to cure him of his gambling addiction.

Her plan begins to unravel when he begins a winning streak on a series of long-shot horses. Soon Lana is on the hook for thousands of dollars; sells her jewelry and furnishings from their penthouse to pay him back. Flood then begins making winning bets for a pair of local judges.

The betting arouses the suspicions of a syndicate mobster, played by Walter Matthau, who demands to know "who's got the action?" When he catches on to the Floods, a team of thugs show up at their apartment, where they find out that Melanie Flood is the "bookie."

In the end, Flood manages to save his marriage and clears his wife of her $18,000 in gambling setbacks through a bit of romance and legal maneuvering.

Production began in January 1962, and some saw the Lana and Dean pairing an "odd couple." Others felt the casting would only add to the wackiness of the story. The fact that director Mann was better known for dramas like *I'll Cry Tomorrow*, *Butterfield 8*, and *The Rose Tattoo* gave producers some concern. Mann himself had no reservations about doing the film. "I figured, Jesus, that's beautiful," recalled Mann, who also had a cut of the proceeds. "I'll get away from something heavy and I'll do a little comedy, which I would love to do. My origins were in the borscht circuit. I was a musician – New York, the Catskills."

Mann enjoyed working on the picture and found Dean easy to work with. "Never any problems with Dean, never any problems in terms of temperament or bullshit or anything else. It couldn't have been nicer," he said. "We would go back to his dressing room, instead

of going to the Paramount commissary. Jay Gerard would organize some Italian food. We'd have a banquet for Christsake." Gerard was best known as Dean's double on the set in many of his pictures.

Lana attended one of Dean's lunchtime gatherings during the filming, but was not impressed. "Dean kept urging me to join his group for lunch, which he usually took in the bungalow reserved for him on the lot. I went there once to find the place filled with his cronies."

Lana claimed Dean's lunches would stretch into two or three hours and that alcohol flowed freely. While many assumed Dean Martin was a heavy drinker; in reality, he was rarely drunk and used it more at a part of his act for his performances. Dean was a relaxed performer who never took himself or his work too seriously. In addition to excursions to golf when he had the chance, Dean also liked to play poker and many of the cast and crew, including Lana, got

Dean and Lana in a scene from the film.

involved in the games. Lana claimed that the long lunches would result in her having to work late on the film. "… Dean strolled onto the set as though he had just decided to drop in on us. All the director could do to make up for lost time was to keep us working well into the evening. Late again!"

Lana's costumes were designed by Edith Head. She had a custom fitted negligee dyed to match her skin tone for several scenes. In addition to the major cast members, a number of notable names signed on for smaller supporting roles, including Nita Talbot, Jack Albertson, John McGiver, and Dan Tobin. Betty Bronson, best known for her 1925 performance as Hollywood's first *Peter Pan*, was cast in a small role as well, but production delays caused her scenes to be scrapped, and they were never put on film.

One cause of the production delays was Lana. While some see comedy as a breeze, other actors find it much more difficult due to the timing and banter of the dialogue. Lana wasn't a natural comedian and had to work hard to keep up with the likes of Dean Martin, Walter Matthau, Nita Talbot and Eddie Albert. In early February, the cast and crew surprised her on her birthday with a party on the set. It was her forty-first birthday and while Lana was happy at the warm reception, the idea of getting older was not something she embraced. During the party, Lana collapsed from exhaustion and spent time at home resting before heading back to work. Cheryl recalled Lana telling her she hadn't been feeling well and that "the birthday toast apparently had a bad effect on her."

Lana eventually returned to work, and the film wrapped by early spring of 1962. Many of the scenes were filmed on location in luxurious penthouse apartments in the historic Talmadge building on Wilshire Boulevard, which fit the bill as the home for the Floods. In addition, a number of driving sequences take place up and down Wilshire Boulevard in downtown Los Angeles. The story's author, Alexander Rose, had a minor cameo role in the film as Mr. Goody.

While Lana was reduced to playing not much more than a housewife for the film, her looks gave the writers a chance to make her the unrequited love of Eddie Albert in the film, allowing viewers to see how he falls for her antics and agrees to help her in her unlikely proposal. Lana got another sexy scene when they dropped her into a bathtub sequence as she played bookie. It would mark her fourth appearance bathing - with previous scenes in *Ziegfeld Girl, The Merry Widow* and *Lady Takes a Flyer*.

Released on December 25 1962, the romantic comedy pulled in a respectable $1.6 million at the box office over the Christmas season. Critics were mixed about the picture. While some felt that the concept held promise, the resulting picture got lost in translation. However, not all the reviews were bad. *Time* magazine wrote that, "The syndicate has the last laugh in this yak derby, but the customers get most of the others …*Who's Got the Action?* is not the merriest oatsmobile that ever came down the track, but Dean and Lana make a surprisingly smooth entry."

Time said that Walter Matthau had some of the better comedic

moments, but that "The whole cast obviously enjoyed making the picture, and most spectators will find that the pleasure is mutual."

However, all was not rosy with Lana on the marriage front. Her days with Fred May were coming to an end. She would file for divorce in October 1962. Lana recalled that May had been acting "morose, uncommunicative, withdrawn," and she had to pry to figure out what was wrong.

Though she feared it might be another woman, he finally admitted it was financial troubles, and he was in need of $5,000 because all his money was tied up in other business dealings. Lana offered to loan him the money and he at first refused. Lana persisted, and he eventually took the money. A short time later, while out to dinner one evening, May surprised Lana with a gift of a brand new Cadillac. So worried about his financial troubles, Lana flew into a rage that he had spent money he didn't have – or her money – on a gift that she didn't want. Possibly reminding her of similar gifts from Johnny Stompanato that she had paid for herself. The two had a huge blow-up argument over the gift, and Lana stormed off to Mexico for a quickie divorce.

TWENTY THREE

"For me, the goal is always to make the page disappear and speak to my reader face to face as each character comes to life."

- Harold Robbins

Lana has to face her demons head on as Harrold Robbins writes a "fictional" version of the tragic events of April 4, 1958, as Lana and Cheryl struggle to put the past behind them.

WHERE HAS LOVE GONE?

If Lana thought that the scandal of 1958 was behind her, she was reminded in 1962 that it was still very much alive.

Simon and Schuster's publishing of Harold Robbins novel, *Where Has Love Gone*, had many readers recognizing striking similarities between the real saga of Lana, Johnny and Cheryl and the fictional tale told in the book. While Lana refused to take the bait, there was little she could do legally with enough of the facts shifted to avoid any real case for cashing in on the tragedy. The book became a bestseller, proving people were very much interested in even a fictional telling of the tale.

The loosely-based story centers on a man named Luke Carey who is trying to start over, with a new wife and a baby on the way, when his past catches up with him after he learns that his fourteen-year-old daughter, whom he hasn't seen in six years, is accused of killing the lover of his ex-wife.

Book reviews immediately saw the similarities between Lana's past and the fictional tale. Robbins and the publisher tried to avoid the references. Robbins found it hard not to admit the scandal played a part is his idea for the story, but felt his books all focused on similar dramatic events. "For me, the goal is always to make the page disappear and speak to my reader face to face as each character comes to life," he told one interviewer.

The success of the novel caused Hollywood to take notice, and Paramount Pictures bought the film rights and hired producer Joseph E. Levine and his production studio, Embassy Pictures, to film the glossy re-telling of the story.

Founded in 1942, Levine's studio had pulled off a similar treatment for Robbins' earlier 1961 novel *The Carpetbaggers*. The film version of *The Carpetbaggers* was a huge hit, earning nearly $29 million with its April 1964 release. Levine hoped *Where Has Love Gone* would garner similar attention.

For *Where Has Love Gone,* achieving that goal would be tricky. Hollywood needed to walk a fine line in trying to capture the real life scandal that rocked Tinsel Town, while avoiding any direct line in suggesting that the soap opera was a retelling of the Lana Turner-Johnny Stompanato affair.

To accomplish this feat it needed a leading lady that could pull off the drama without coming off like Lana Turner. Susan Hayward fit the bill, and since the story focused largely on the role of the father, Mike Conners' character helped differentiate the real scandal from the big screen feature. Bette Davis also took part, adding additional luster to the feature. Joey Heatherton took on the "Cheryl Crane" character, playing the daughter who murdered her mother's lover. The movie version stripped away any references to the father's new life and focused on the family drama and court proceedings surrounding the murder.

While the producers hoped for the best in teaming Hayward and Davis, many feared that the pair was doomed. Davis' recent behavior on the set of *What Ever Happened to Baby Jane?*, with Joan Crawford, and Crawford's exit from the follow-up film, *Hush ... Hush, Sweet Charlotte*, had many expecting the worst. Battling Davis was becoming commonplace for any woman who starred alongside her. Sadly, they weren't wrong when Hayward and Davis came head to head in disagreements over the script.

To promote the film, the producers denied any connection to the Lana Turner tale and tried to tie the film to the success of their

Cliff Robertson and Lana in a scene from "Love Has Many Faces."

other 1964 hit. "From the blistering best-seller! From the team that brought you *'The Carpetbaggers'*! The explosive story of the violent world where a mother and her teenage daughter compete for the same lover...*WHERE LOVE HAS GONE* goes where no motion picture has ever dared go before!"

Where Has Love Gone didn't garner the critical or financial success of *The Carpetbaggers*, only pulling in about $3.6 million. Even Bette Davis' *Hush ... Hush, Sweet Charlotte*, released the same year, out-grossed the film. While *The Carpetbaggers* became the fourth highest grossing picture of 1964, *Where Has Love Gone* didn't even make the top 25.

The Saturday Review criticized the script, saying that it "somehow manages to make every dramatic line (particularly when uttered by Susan Hayward) sound like a caption to a cartoon in *The New Yorker*.

Newsweek found *Where Has Love Gone* a bit disappointing, calling the film "a typical Harold Robbins pastiche of newspaper clippings liberally shellacked with sentiment and glued with sex. ... The gang at Embassy and Paramount are probably congratulating themselves on their monumental restraint and good taste – simply because they didn't try to cast Lana Turner in the leading role."

Both Lana and Cheryl read the book when it came out, but never spoke of it to the press, not wanting to make any unnecessary connections than the casual reader already might have made. Lana refused to see the film or to give the media a chance to rehash an event that she had been trying hard to put behind her. Cheryl, however, admitted sneaking into a theater after the film's release in November 1964. Sitting "slumped down as low as possible" she recalled "cringing for nearly two hours before slipping out of the theater," as she drew connections between her own past and the story unfolding on the big screen.

Lana, on the other hand, didn't spend a whole lot of time focusing on the Hayward-Davis drama. Rather, she was busy working on her own film. After turning down Ross Hunter's offer to star in *The Chalk Garden*, Lana accepted the lead in *Love Has Many Faces*.

Lana in a scene from the film.

The feature would hit movie screens in early 1965 just months after *Where Has Love Gone* debuted. While it cost considerably less to make than the Paramount release, Lana's own drama didn't win fans over either, pulling in only about $1.1 million in the United States.

Love Has Many Faces cast Lana as a wealthy older woman drawing attention from a host of younger men in the luxurious tropical setting of Acapulco. When an American beach boy washes up dead on a beach, police suspect murder. When they find out that the victim was a gigolo, a host of suspects arise including Turner's character and her current male lover, played by Cliff Robertson.

Released by Columbia Pictures, the film was directed by Alexander Singer, written by Marguerite Roberts and included a title song from Nancy Wilson. Moreover, Edith Head designed Lana Turner's clothes, dressing her in everything from she chic pantsuits to evening gowns and bathing suits.

The story opens with a dead American "beach boy" washing up on a beach in Acapulco. A police investigation suspects murder, and police lieutenant Riccardo Andrade of the Mexican police has three suspects – Hank Walker, played by Hugh O'Brian, another beach boy gigolo who blackmails vacationing older women; Pete Jordan, played by Cliff Robertson, another former beach boy who is married to suspect number three, a rich American beauty named Kit, played by Lana. Police discover that Kit had an affair with the dead man, and the remainder of the story focuses on the search for the truth and the lives of those impacted by the investigation. Stefanie Powers earned a supporting role as the former girlfriend of the dead beach boy who comes to town looking for the truth.

The film was the final picture for Cliff Robertson, who was under contract with Columbia, and was eager to end his association with the studio. Stephanie Powers was also a contract player for the studio who had hoped the movie might be a good one to help her early in her career. Powers called the film a "love square" between the characters and said that "should have given us a clue to the impending disaster." She recalled it as "one of the best bad movies ever made."

Lana loved Acapulco, and it was easy to convince her to do the film once the location was presented to her. Local homes were used for sets and Lana had a chance to relax in the sun in between shooting. Even her mother visited her while at work. Lana also had memories of Johnny in Acapulco, but decided to put them to rest buy

making new memories. One particular fascination she developed was around bullfighting. She became a fan and then friends with many of the bullfighters and found herself invited to all the major fights. Many of the bullfighters were attracted to Lana too, and she had a few bulls dedicated to her when she attended the fights. She even found a date or two from a few of the eligible bachelors behind the red cape. Jaime Bravo, was one of the fighters that Lana was drawn to. She even managed to get him into the film, *Love Has Many Faces,* with a small cameo.

The script lacked cohesion and planned rewrites never happened, leaving actors frustrated with the meandering story. In addition, the heat, and challenge of filming on the remote location, made it confusing and difficult to capture the necessary footage. After weeks on location, the film wrapped and everyone headed back to Hollywood to finish the picture.

Lana promoted the picture by appearing in a short documentary feature called *Million Dollar Wardrobe.* Used to promote both the theatrical and television releases of *Love Has Many Faces*, the film focused on Edith Head's costumes for Lana and other stars of the film. Lana is featured modeling a number of the costumes from the movie along with Stefanie Powers. Scenes of costars Cliff Robertson, Ruth Roman and Hugh O'Brian from the Acapulco filming also are included. Powers felt that Lana got all the good costumes, and she was handed what didn't distract from the star of the picture. "Miss Head chose to clothe me entirely in beige so that I blended nicely with the background. Lana, on the other hand, was resplendent in costumes of aquamarine, chiffon, sequins and shocking pink."

Lana reportedly became friends with Stefanie Powers, who was at the beginning of her career. Some found it surprising that Lana didn't distance herself from a much younger, and beautiful actress by whom she might have felt threatened.

Powers found Lana to be "a vulnerable beauty, and in her eyes I saw an unexpected childlike innocence. She worried about everything, and so nervous that the silk of her dress would quiver from the tremor of her body."

Lana's press agent George Nichols, recalled the experience as a bit difficult for the leading lady. "Lana was drinking during *Love Has Many Faces*. Acapulco reminded her of the past - the good and the bad times. It was difficult for me to believe Lana drank during working hours, but she did. Lana had flings, but she was very lonely ... a frightened child. Alcohol gave her the confidence to face life every day."

After returning from Acapulco, Lana took up with another young handsome actor named Robert Eaton. A decade younger than her, Lana told friends he was the first man to ever satisfy her in bed. She told tales of her sexual conquests and of spending days locked in the bedroom making love to him. The two were married on June 22, 1965 at his family's home in Arlington, Virginia. The marriage would last until 1969.

Eaton arrived in Hollywood like so many others, with hopes of stardom. As an actor, his career fizzled, but when he met Lana he fashioned himself as a producer. Unlike Johnny, this time Lana helped set him up in her production company. However, the projects never materialized. While Lana spent her money on keeping Eaton living the good life, he reportedly spent his efforts on the attentions of other women. After returning from a trip abroad, Lana found out that Eaton had been cheating on her in her own house and bed and kicked him out. Yet, it never took Lana long to find the next man – one was usually waiting just around the bend.

Twenty Four

"It's said in Hollywood that you should always forgive your enemies - because you never know when you'll have to work with them."

- Lana Turner

Lana tackles a grand production remake of a famous play and film. It would prove to be a challenging task, but a role she would consider one of her proudest moments.

MADAME X

Regardless of Lana's personal tragedies, the notoriety of her private life became less and less of an anchor in the years following the Stompanato killing. The fact was Lana was an aging actress in a business focused on the young. While still beautiful and talented, good scripts became harder and harder to come by. It wasn't that Lana didn't receive offers, but like her last few films, the quality of the projects was often questionable.

The reality was that Hollywood was changing and actresses from its heyday - leading ladies like Joan Crawford, Bette Davis, Barbara Stanwyck and Olivia de Havilland - were all finding it difficult to get good parts. Younger actresses like Audrey Hepburn, Lee Remick, Julie Andrews, Julie Christie and Joanne Woodward were landing the meatier roles that Lana might have coveted.

By 1962, Lana had set up her own production company and bought the rights to *Madame X* with plans to remake the lush tale along the lines of *Imitation of Life*. Acquired from MGM, *Madame X* is based on a 1909 French play by Alexandre Bisson. It was first filmed in 1916, with Dorothy Donnelly as its star. A remake in 1920 starred Pauline Frederick, and in 1929, the first version with sound earned an Academy Award nomination for its star Ruth Chatterton. It was remade again in 1937 by MGM with Gladys George in the title role. A British version was even filmed in 1948.

For the modern day update, Lana entered into a co-production deal with Ross Hunter. But it would take three years for Hunter and writer Jean Holloway to pen a script Lana found acceptable. Hunter initially wanted Douglas Sirk to direct the film, capturing the same gloss as so many of his past hits. Sirk, in poor health, was unable to accept, choosing instead to retire from filmmaking. David Lowell Rich was hired instead. Rich was an unusual choice in some ways because his background was nearly entirely in television. However, his broad variety and extensive resume showed he could tackle the project. Having worked on TV shows like *The Alfred Hitchcock Hour, Twilight Zone, Route 66, Dr. Kildare, Ben Casey, Wagon Train, Peter Gunn* and *The Barbara Stanwyck Show*, the producers knew he had the skills to pull off the project. As for Hunter, the choice was not unusual as he was known for keeping production costs low by avoiding high-salaried directors when possible.

It wasn't until 1965 that *Madame X* went before the cameras and Lana was 44-years old. Aside from the fact that she hadn't had a starring role that required her to appear in nearly every scene in years, she also faced the challenge of having to age from 30 to 55 in the span of two hours.

Lana plays Holly, the wife of a U.S. diplomat, played by John Forsythe, and the mother of a young son. Neglected by his long and frequent absences, she has an affair with the town playboy, played by Ricardo Montalban. When she ends the affair, her lover pushes back and during a struggle he falls down a flight of stairs to his death. Holly leaves the scene of the crime, hoping to avoid a scandal, but her mother-in-law has her followed and comes up with incriminating evidence against her. With her son's political career at risk, Lana's mother-in-law, played by Constance Bennett, forces Holly to fake her own death and leave town, leaving her husband and son behind to grieve her. As the years go by, Holly is haunted by the life she left behind, and uses alcohol to numb the pain. When a con man, played by Burgess Meredith, discovers her secret and attempts to blackmail her, he too ends up dead. Holly, now known only as Madame X, ends up on trial for his murder, ironically being defended by the son she gave up some 20 years earlier, but he has no idea who she is.

If Lana had any concerns that the subject matter would open old wounds of the Johnny Stompanato scandal, she didn't show it. Still, many saw her personal life as a backdrop of the drama on the big screen. With her lover murdered and threats of public ruin and scandal, it was hard not to see elements of her personal story in the film. But Lana ignored any suggestion that her personal life had anything to do with the selection of the project. It was a good role, and Lana found them few and far between and was happy to have a chance to take part in a quality picture.

Filming took place primarily in Los Angeles. Cheryl even recalled that the house used for the early scenes was just down the block from a home she lived in as a child. The house would later become Hugh Hefner's Playboy Mansion. Producers were permitted to film only the front of the house from the driveway to the mailbox. Interiors were shot on a Hollywood soundstage.

Early in production, Lana seemed to be enjoying herself. Some say that was not surprising considering her character was a young and glamorous woman dressed in a gorgeous Jean Louis wardrobe and draped in jewels. Those on the set felt that as her character aged, Lana's interest in the film and character deteriorated. In her mid-40s, Lana was all too aware and self-conscious about aging, and her spirits were dampened by the unflattering makeup she was forced to endure as her character aged. There were reported feuds with her long-time friend and makeup man Del Armstrong, who insisted she look as haggard and old as the script called for, Lana called for restraint. Cheryl claimed that her mother didn't want her to come to the set so she didn't have to see her in her "ugly makeup."

"When I thought he'd made me look horrible enough, he said 'You ain't seen nothing yet,' and he meant it," Lana said. "I mean, I've had some bad mornings in my time, but I've never looked like that!"

Lana was so distressed by her appearance that she insisted on wearing a veil while walking to and from the set. Cheryl recalled that Lana did retain some of her own vanity by having "perfectly manicured nails" during the emotional climatic scenes her aged character is dying with her son by her side. She asked her mother about it after seeing the film. Lana claimed that it must have been an over-sight of her having to film a scene where her character was younger followed by an older-aged scene.

Lana hit the roof when columnist Sheilah Graham visited the set and reported that Constance Bennett, who played Lana's mother-in-law, looked younger than Lana. Bennett was in her late fifties, and Lana wasn't wearing her old-age makeup on the day of Graham's

visit.

Others say Lana also engaged in arguments with Ross Hunter over the script and production. After he had accused Lana of causing costly delays to production Lana flew into a rage. Hunter threw up his arms and stomped off the set refusing to speak to Lana for the remainder of the picture. Filming reportedly took about eight weeks and gossip columnists got wind of the feud; but star and producer both denied there was anything to the stories. After completion

of the film, Lana took out ads in Hollywood trade papers thanking Hunter and the 75-member cast and crew for helping her through the difficult role.

Critics called *Madame X* "hopelessly old-fashioned," but not all the reviews were bad. Some praised the film, calling Lana's performance harrowing. Critic for the *Independent Film Journal,* Abe Greenberg, and Dorothy Manners of *The New York Times* suggested that Lana might have found herself nominated for an Academy Award had the film done better at the box office. Charles Champlin of *The Los Angeles Times* wrote that the "unsparing, guileless honesty of her performance is very touching."

James Powers of *The Hollywood Reporter* wrote, "A superb cast of players take this rather shabby old piece and gives it immediacy, vigor and credibility."

By the time of the film's premiere in March 1966, Lana had a facelift, possibly wanting to dispel any rumors that she looked anything like the tragic figure at the close of the picture. The procedure was a heavily guarded secret, and only a few people knew she'd had any work done.

Lana would deny using the services of a plastic surgeon to retain her looks as the years went by. And *Madame X,* even with all the difficulty and drama surrounding it, would remain one of her personal favorites. She would often tell people it was one of the performances of which she was most proud.

Lana was also proud of the fact that internationally the filmed also earned strong reviews. She was awarded the David Di Donatello Award for "Best Foreign Actress" at the Taormina Film Festival in Italy, as well as La Perla Verde (the Green Pearl Trophy) by the theater owners of Italy.

TWENTY
FIVE

"People who have it all, and want more."

> *- The Survivors,*
> *ABC Television*

When the feature film roles grow scarce, Lana takes to the small screen in a nighttime soap opera, but finds it takes more than glamour to keep the show afloat.

LANA TAKES TO THE SMALL SCREEN

After *Madame X*, Lana was without a project to sink her teeth into. She had been offered a role in a film tentatively titled "Shocking!" but rejected the script. The plan was to have her star alongside Ava Gardner or Rita Hayworth as sisters out to kill each other. Along the lines of *What Ever Happened to Baby Jane?*, the film was intended to take a pair of glamorous leading ladies and drop them into the world of low-budget horrors, but none of the actresses was willing to take part. Another project, announced in 1966, would had Lana working with Federico Fellini in a film called "North to Brindisi," but again, the project fell through.

As the 1960s came to a close, no new film offers were coming her way, but when ABC television announced its 1969 fall line-up, a familiar face would be landing on TV screens each week. Lana Turner would make her debut in her first TV series - *The Survivors*.

Lana had seldom appeared on TV during her career, feeling that her movie star image might be downgraded by showing up on the small screen. When her hit movie *Peyton Place* was turned into a glossy nighttime soap opera in 1964, Lana was nowhere to be found. In fact, none of the stars of the original film showed up. Dorothy Malone took on Lana's Constance MacKenzie role, and a band of up and coming actors, including Mia Farrow, Ryan O'Neal and Barbara Parkins, took up the major roles. The series quickly became a hit, running from 1964 until 1969. In fact, during its debut, it aired twice a week and did so well in the ratings that ABC increased it to three nights a week. ABC suspected that another nighttime soap, featuring a glamour queen of Lana's stature could be a surefire hit. To lure her, they had to offer her a larger salary, star billing and to assure her she'd look every bit as glamorous on the small screen as she used to on the big one.

When Lana was approached to tackle TV this time she agreed in part due to the money as well as the chance to work. The fact that she would be dressed in gowns, furs and jewels each week also didn't hurt. However, many were surprised by her association with the show due to the man who helped create it.

The Survivors was based on a story by bestselling author Harold Robbins, the same man who had crafted *Where Has Love Gone*, the story that held striking similarities to the Johnny Stompanato events of a decade earlier. Lana refused to discuss the book or the film when it was released in the mid-60s, but it didn't escape Hollywood that Robbins had used the sensational drama of Lana's past to further his own success.

ABC put a lot of hope in the high-profile show, hoping the glamorous new prime time soap opera starring Lana Turner would draw in the viewers. It received strong promotion when the network announced its fall lineup. In addition to Turner, a host of other familiar faces, including Kevin McCarthy, George Hamilton, Jan-Michael Vincent, Ralph Bellamy, Diana Muldaur, and Natalie Schafer took part.

It first aired on September 29, 1969 with much hype. It would limp along in the ratings until its final episode on January 12, 1970. Each episode basically captured a chapter of Robbins' story. ABC had given the series a green light, committing to 26 episodes but despite all the promotion, the series was a loser in primetime ratings. *The Survivors* would actually only air 15 episodes, trailing badly behind *Mayberry R.F.D.* and *The Doris Day Show* on CBS and *The NBC Monday Movie*. Roughly halfway in, the network began looking for ways to pull the plug rather than continue producing more costly

episodes.

Since the show was serialized, the network felt it had little chance of drawing in new viewers once the plot started to unravel, and new viewers wouldn't be able to catch up. Since it included a large cast of characters, it was quite expensive to produce. The budget was nearly $250,000 per episode, and ABC needed strong ratings to garner the advertising dollars to keep the show afloat. When

Lana closed out the 60s with a role in "The Big Cube."

it failed to deliver, it was cancelled in midseason. ABC would rerun the episodes the following summer in an effort to recoup some of its investment, but again the series failed to lure in viewers. The show's reviews were largely negative and there were rumors of production problems, including a clash between Lana and three of the show's producers that would lead to their being fired.

A November 10, 1969 issue of the industry news journal *Broadcasting* reported that ABC would move the series midseason from Monday nights at 9 p.m. to Thursday at 10 p.m. *Broadcasting* then reported a week later that although ABC committed to a full season of *The Survivors* from Universal "weak ratings and disastrous reviews, is expected to announce drastic change in format for series starting at midseason."

When the reboot was announced, the magazine reported that the "key ingredient to be held over would be series co-star George Hamilton. Lana Turner and Kevin McCarthy will be dropped."

In December, it was announced that the producers would stick with George Hamilton but would jettison everything else from the series and create a completely new program. The new series that debuted was called *Paris 7000* and starred Hamilton as Jack Brennan, a diplomat working at the American embassy in Paris. Although ratings were marginally better than *The Survivors* and the show was less expensive to produce, the show was cancelled at the end of the season after only seven episodes.

Aside from television, Lana also accepted a part in a big screen feature, when she starred in 1969's *The Big Cube*. Released by Warner Bros., the suspense thriller was directed by Tito Davison and starred Lana opposite Karin Mossberg, George Chakiris, Daniel O'Herlihy and Richard Egan. It would mark one of Lana's final big screen appearances, but its limited release left a lot of people unaware Lana had actually even made the film. Any press and attention it did get was mostly because of the film's focus on the use of LSD during the late 1960s. Suggesting that drug use leads to only evil, the story puts Lana through the ringer as the victim of a troubled cast of characters.

Lana plays Adriana Roman, a successful actress who retires from the stage in order to marry Charles Winthrop, a wealthy tycoon played by Daniel O'Herlihy. Her new teenage step-daughter, Lisa, played by Karin Mossberg, distrusts Adriana and resents her for stealing her father's affection.

After Winthrop is killed in a boating accident, Adriana inherits his estate and wields control over his daughter's inheritance. Her stepdaughter's drug-making boyfriend, played by George Chakiris, convinces Lisa to get rid of Adriana by tricking her into taking LSD to drive her insane. Once Adriana is committed, the estate would become the daughter's and she and her boyfriend could make off with the fortune.

In the end, Lisa saves Adriana, realizing she's not the villain after all, and her boyfriend is the far bigger threat. In order to help Adriana recover from amnesia, her friend and playwright Frederick, played by Richard Egan, devises a way to help cure her. He writes a play detailing Adriana's traumatic experiences and casts her in the lead role. By the time the play opens, Adriana is having flashbacks to her past, but doesn't yet understand where the play and her real life begin and end. By the close of the play and some dramatic efforts on the part of Lisa and Frederick, Lana is on the road to recovery. Cheryl recalled that she "couldn't believe her eyes" after seeing another film of Lana's focusing on a deadly mother-daughter relationship that carried reminders of her own past.

The feature was filmed in Mexico by ANCO Productions during May and June of 1968. The Acapulco location might have again been the lure to get Lana to agree to do the film. Lana also was pleased to find herself dressed in gowns by William Travilla for much of the picture. Travilla was best known for costuming Marilyn Monroe in features like *Gentlemen Prefer Blondes, How to Marry a Millionaire* and *The Seven Year Itch*.

The Big Cube would be a joint release by Warner Bros and Seven Arts and found some success with showings in Boston, Cleveland and Chicago, but it didn't really garner a lot of attention in the press and was overshadowed by a host of bigger pictures that year. Corporate shuffling at Warner Bros. also left the film out to dry, where it and many other films failed due to a lack of distribution. It fared better south of the border in a dubbed version of the picture.

"The Big Cube" had Lana being tricked into taking LSD in an event to drive her crazy by a wicked stepdaughter.

TWENTY SIX

"The truth is, sex doesn't mean that much to me now."

- Lana Turner

Lana plays a 40-year-old divorcee who has a rejuvenating affair with a younger man in Jay Allen's adaptation of a Pierre Barillet and Jean-Pierre Gredy comedic play.

.

THE STAGE BECKONS

By the 1970s Lana's career was in decline. While financially she was in no need of work, she continued to look for opportunities to reach her fans and garner the attention a star enjoys. When those opportunities didn't come in the form of film or television scripts, she surprisingly found offers on the stage.

Opening on June 8, 1971, *Forty Carats* would mark Lana's first live stage performance. With a ten-week tour through Washington, Baltimore, New York, Philadelphia and Chicago, Lana took on the starring role of a glamorous 40 year-old divorcee who falls in love with a man 18-years her junior. Julie Harris earned a Tony Award for her version on Broadway in 1969.

Lana was at first fearful of the idea of appearing in front of a live audience. Although she appeared before crowds on Bob Hope's USO tours, her biggest live performance to date had been back in 1958 on the witness stand after the death of Johnny Stompanato. In films, she knew there was always a second take, along with lighting and make-up to make her look her best. If she flubbed her lines on stage, it was there for everyone to see. However, the producers were persistent, offering her the best star accommodations and a paycheck of $17,500 a week for 10 weeks. That was good enough for Lana, but the best selling factors were the 14 fabulous gowns designed for her to wear by Nolan Miller.

As opening night grew closer, Lana began to grow more and more fearful of her debut. Those around her noticed her drinking more than usual to get through her rehearsals. One evening she reportedly called a friend drunk, babbling into the phone that she "couldn't go through with it." Fearing for her health and safety, the friend called the police and an ambulance, thinking Lana might be considering taking her own life. Lana was embarrassed when paramedics arrived at her New York hotel room. She had to explain that she was merely fearful of her debut and didn't think she could go through with opening night in New York.

Though she was terrified of the live performances she was also disappointed at the fact that she didn't get the complete star treatment she was expecting. During her hotel stay, Lana was expecting limousines to take her to and from rehearsals and was shocked to find she had to make her own way to the theater each day. Producers explained that Broadway wasn't Hollywood, and it was common for actors to walk through the streets of New York or even take a taxi. Lana wasn't happy but managed to make do. When asked by the press about the role, she said, "When I got the call about *Forty Carats,* I assumed it was a movie, but I was tired of sitting around. I thought doing a play would be a challenge."

While Lana enjoyed the attention the show brought her, critics were mixed over her performance. Many said it was Lana Turner playing Lana Turner. Some found her glamour reminiscent of Hollywood's days gone by, while others found it pretentious. When the story found its way to film in 1973, Lana was reportedly not considered for the leading role in the feature film version.

When the film roles were hard to find Lana took to the stage in the 1970s.

Still, the success of *Forty Carats* would lead to several more live performances during the decade. In the spring of 1975, Lana agreed to a one-night only appearance in New York's Town Hall in her honor. It was part of a special series of events where Hollywood writer and publicist John Springer invited legendary ladies of the silver screen to meet fans and answer questions in a live performance. A screening of movie clips would introduce the star, and the evening would center on her glamorous and exciting career. Joan Crawford, Bette Davis, Ginger Rogers and Rosalind Russell were a few of the leading ladies to appear. Lana was perhaps the youngest legend to take part and enjoyed the attention the evening brought.

Lana would follow up her April Town Hall appearance with another live show in November 1975, when she agreed to star in *The Pleasure of His Company*, opposite Louis Jourdan at the Arlington Park Theater in Chicago. Originally booked for a three-week run, the show was extended four more weeks after strong demand for tickets. Reports suggested that the play would have been extended again except for the fact that Jourdan had another project to which he was committed, and Lana refused to continue with another actor.

If Lana had forgotten about the nightmare surrounding Johnny Stompanato by the early 70s, she had a small reminder when Mickey Cohen was released from federal prison in 1972. After 10 years behind bars for income tax violations, Cohen exited prison and began a public campaign for prison reform that got him back into the headlines. He also made headlines again in 1974 when he claimed to be in contact with the captives of Patty Hearst who were asking for a ransom for her release. Lana never mentioned his name again, and Cohen seemed to have put Turner behind him as well. He would die of natural causes in 1976 without ever crossing paths with Lana again.

If the 1970s meant Lana's career slowed, it gave her an opportunity to focus marginally more on the relationship with her daughter. Lana spent the better part of the 60s still trying her hand at a happy marriage. Following the end of her 1960-62 marriage to Fred May she married Robert Eaton in 1965. A younger man, Eaton fancied himself as a producer and Lana helped him professionally as well as financially. Shortly after their divorce she met Ronald Dante, a nightclub hypnotist who reportedly liked Lana's money more than he did her. During a trip to San Francisco, he left Turner and disappeared with a check for $35,000 that she had given him. After his abandoning her, she later accused him of stealing $100,000 worth of jewelry from her home when she was away for a weekend in Palm Springs. No charges were ever filed, and Lana decided it was safer to be celibate than go looking for another husband. Lana gave up on marital bliss after her final marriage to Ronald Dante in 1972.

Without husbands or work Lana had more time to rebuild her relationship with her daughter.

Cheryl and Lana had embarked on a rocky relationship following the death of Johnny Stompanato to say the least. After her time in juvenile hall and her issues with reform school, Cheryl had to grow up fast. The media attention surrounding Johnny's death and life as the daughter of a famous movie star meant it was hard to escape the notoriety her name brought her. After dealing with years of authority figures and the media, Cheryl had had enough of wardens, detention officers, psychiatrists, therapists and the police. She had her share of courtrooms and hearings as well. She spent the remainder of her childhood years being shepherded between reform schools and her grandmother, with an equal share of visits with her father and mother. She had to deal with not only the drama surrounding the death of her mother's lover, but also the sexual assaults she recalled at the hands of her stepfather, Lex Barker. The 60s were a time of rebellion and escape, as well as a search for the person she would become.

Lana and Cheryl saw each other periodically, though it would be hard to call the two close. Cheryl recalled their relationship as "strained, but cordial." They never spoke of the evening of April 4,

1958 at any length once the incident was put behind them and only referred to it as "The Paragraph," because anytime anything was written about either woman, a paragraph on the Stompanato incident was included in the story. Lana said that after Johnny's death and the inquest, "deeper problems surfaced."

"Her defiance had a tough edge that made her impossible to control. For her seventeenth birthday, I had presented her with a Ford Thunderbird. Late at night, she would sneak out of the house to meet friends, and they would roll her car out of the garage and onto the road" … "Fred [May] and I never knew she was gone until one night the police brought her home. They had picked her up wandering alone in a rather notorious place called Tuna Canyon."

After 16 days in juvenile hall, Cheryl was released. Closing in on her adulthood, Cheryl could almost taste freedom, "On release, I still had six months until my eighteenth birthday. That glittering prize was so important to me that I named it 'Free Day' and marked off the remaining days on a wallet calendar."

Cheryl said that although she acted the part of a solid citizen on the surface, inside she was "smoldering with a low sense of self and the same old guilts."

Released to the care of Lana, she recalled having 184 days until she was eighteen.

Adulthood allowed Cheryl to take control of her own life and turn herself around. She eventually went to work for her father in the restaurant business and would become his business partner, thriving in the role and responsibility. Starting as a "seater" at his restaurant, her first job was merely escorting diners to their table. In the hands of her father, she had the opportunity to learn all sides of his restaurant chain. The $10 million business became a career; and after attending school to get a formal education in the restaurant business, she worked her way up to executive vice president.

She would meet her partner Joyce "Josh" LeRoy in 1968 at a party, and the two would begin a long and successful relationship. Cheryl wrote that she found the relationship deepened over time, and she knew eventually she would have to talk about that fateful Good Friday in 1958. Josh responded by telling her she thought it was a brave thing to do in coming to her mother's defense and Cheryl was surprised by her acceptance. "For all these years, I had lived with terrible knowledge that I had killed another human being. It was a notion so overwhelmingly horrible that I had to shut the door on it, bury it away out of sight, in order to get on with my life. The idea of dispassionately considering the whys and wherefores of the deed, no less of concluding that it was anything but deplorable, was simply beyond me."

But Cheryl concluded that finding someone to share her story with – and ultimately her life with – changed her. She said that in the coming weeks, Josh encouraged her to speak the name Stompanato "until the sting went out of it."

After dealing with the tragedy of Good Friday for a decade, Cheryl had finally begun to come to terms with the events.

Once in the care of her grandmother, Cheryl found that Lana's mother, Mildred, was getting older and no longer able to live on her own. With the tables turned, she and Josh moved Gran in with them, setting up an apartment for her in their home. She and Lana however, were not all that close during the 70s, with Lana once telling her, "I'm sorry. I just don't remember a lot of the 70s."

Lana, aside from the travel of work on the road, found alcohol a comfort and way to dull the loneliness and pain of growing older alone. In 1971, Lana met a hairdresser and former Arthur Murray dance instructor named Eric Root. Root would become Lana's personal stylist and sometimes escort. He also claimed to be her confidant - so much so that he claimed that she confessed to him that she was, in fact, the one who killed Johnny Stompanato.

"We were sitting in our suite at the Plaza Hotel, watching a documentary on Hollywood Scandals," wrote Root. "Suddenly images of Lana, Johnny Stompanato and Cheryl flashed across the screen."

"Lana, do you want me to turn it off?" I asked.

"No," she said. She watched the rest of the story and turned off the set once the show moved onto another scandal. He said she became "agitated and angry," but that the two didn't speak for some time, until she eventually blurted out, "I killed the son of a bitch and I'd do it again."

"What?" Root asked.

"Scratch that," she said.

Root would claim that several hours later Lana confided further in him, telling him, "If I die before my daughter, you should tell the truth so that I can rest in peace. Don't let my baby take the rap all her life for my mistake … Now you know, I've spoken to you, and said things I've never told anyone else, until tonight."

However, Cheryl discounted the claim, saying, "This idea that Root had in his book is so far-fetched … You know, everybody has something they want to sell. I guess it was the only way he could get the book published."

The film roles were few and far between in the 1970s with Lana finding one acting role in the 1974 British thriller *Persecution*. Retitled in some markets as *The Terror of Sheba* or *The Graveyard*, the film was directed by Don Chaffey.

The story centers on a young man named David Masters who drowns his mother's Persian cat, Sheba, in a bowl of milk. His anger stems from a belief that his mother loves her cats more than him, so he takes out his anger by killing each of her cats. He returns home years later as a grown man, looking to restart his relationship with his mother. Along with him come his wife and newborn child. His mother, played by Lana, vows revenge on him and decides to toy with him like a cat playing with a mouse. The spiral of vengeance leads ultimately to tragedy. In addition to Lana, the film stars Ralph Bates, Trevor Howard and Suzan Farmer.

The film did little at the box office. Aside from the confusion surrounding the title changes, a lot of bigger markets didn't carry the film. Released in the United Kingdom in 1974 and in the United States in the fall of 1975 by several small distribution houses, few saw the film, and Lana received very little notice for having acted in it at all.

Lana would get another offer for a film after *Persecution* when she took on the role of Claire in the drama *Bittersweet Love*. Released in 1976, *Bittersweet Love* costarred Robert Lansing, Celeste Holm, Robert Alda, Meredith Baxter Birney, and Scott Hylands, the story about recounts a young couple who meet, fall in love, and get married. When the couple discover that they are pregnant, drama ensues when they discover that they are actually brother and sister. His father had an affair years ago with her mother and she, the daughter, just happened to meet her brother years later. Lana plays the mother holding

the long kept secret that tears her apart and threatens the happiness of her entire family. The film received little notice and was panned by critics.

Lana also did a bit more theater work in the latter part of the decade, appearing in a touring production of *Bell, Book and Candle* that made stops in Michigan, New Jersey, Upstate New York, Colorado, Maine, New Hampshire and Pennsylvania. She also agreed to appear at Drury Lane Theater in Chicago in a production of *Divorce Me, Darling*.

As for her former husband, Stephen Crane sold his hotel chain in 1978 and retired, while Cheryl and her partner Josh moved to Hawaii. Cheryl took up a second career in real estate. After spending about a year living in a retirement community, Gran was convinced to relocate to Hawaii with Cheryl. Lana began to visit and mother and daughter would start to build a new relationship.

"As it turned out, the Lana Turner who stepped off the plane in Hawaii was no one we knew. She was so easy-going and good-natured that after an exchange of sly smiles, Josh and I stopped calling her 'Mother.' That was much too formal. She was now 'Mom.' "

Cheryl had always found that her mother's stardom created a "Lana Turner" that the star felt the public demanded, and as the years went by, the line between the real Lana Turner and the star became blurry. Even referring to her at times as L.T., Cheryl could often notice the change between public and private Lana. It was one of the traits that may very well have led to the wall between the two women. But Cheryl began to find that Lana, in her aging years, was finally giving way to the person. During her time in Hawaii, Cheryl noticed, "Off came the makeup, except for her lipstick and eyebrows. Gone were the archness of L.T., the sternness of Mother. There were no deep-breathing *Peyton Place* stares, no dramatic pauses as if she were shooting a close-up. This nice lady, Mom, displayed the bounce she had shown the world at nineteen in *Love Finds Andy Hardy*. She spoke straight from the shoulder. She even laughed at herself.

Lana must have liked the person she was in Hawaii as well. She purchased a condo there in order to spend more time with her mother and daughter. She would live there periodically during the course of the next three years.

Early into Lana's stay in Hawaii, her mother's health began to deteriorate, and she required round-the-clock nursing. Lana convinced her it was in her best interest to relocate to a nursing home, and her mother reluctantly agreed. Cheryl called it her mother's "finest hour" and saw it as a strong and selfless act, with no shades of a theatrical performance. When her mother died roughly four months later, they scattered her ashes in Hawaii.

TWENTY SEVEN

"It's all publicity trying to drum up a feud between us."

- Lana Turner

Lana heads off to the fictional vineyards of Northern California for a prime-time soap opera featuring another screen legend for small screen drama in 'Falcon Crest.' And a few last roles would await, along with the chance to tell her story in print.

THE LAST HURRAH

Lana had settled into the twilight years of her career believing that the movie roles and starring performances were long behind her. While she continued to work sporadically during the last decade of her life, the roles were few and far between. She would take to the stage once more in a brief production of *Murder Among Friends* in New Orleans in March 1980, but her biggest undertaking in the early 1980s was at last to pen her autobiography.

Lana said that she had been offered millions over the years to tell her tale. Finally, as the glitter and fame began to recede, her chance to tell her side of her story was one last opportunity to capture the spotlight. *Lana: The Lady, The Legend, The Truth* was published in 1982 and earned mixed reviews for Lana's version of her life story. While some found the telling of her tale long overdue, others felt she left some of the grittier truth between the lines or off the pages entirely. However, interest in the book did generate strong sales and attention for its author.

In 1980 she also found a film role in a remake of Lon Chaney's 1944 film *Weird Woman*. Remade first in 1962 as *Burn, Witch, Burn!*, the latter film, *Witches Brew*, was a horror spoof center-

ing on three women who use witch-craft to help their husbands further their careers. Eventually, the women find themselves competing against each other as they fight for the same role for their husbands at a university where the men are all professors. The film stars Terri Garr, Kathryn Leigh Scott and Kelly Jean Peters as the trio of wives. Richard Benjamin plays Garr's professor husband. Lana portrays Vivian Cross, a socialite with a talent for witchcraft who gets

the story rolling. The film did little to ignite Lana's film career, but it did enable her to keep working until the next opportunity arose. Both Lana and Garr, according to Cheryl, found the movie, "so bad, it's funny."

In addition to the book and film, Lana was photographed for a Blackglama fur fashion ad in 1980, and a short time later, she had the chance to reach a new generation of fans and rewrite a missed opportunity from the late 1960s. Many stars from the golden age of

Hollywood had embraced television and some had launched careers that were even more successful on the small screen than they ever were in movie theaters.

Joan Collins had hopes of being the next Elizabeth Taylor, but ended up little more than a B-movie actress in the 1950s. That would all change in 1981 when she debuted as Alexis Carrington in *Dynasty*. Barbara Bel Geddes would forever be best known as Miss Ellie in *Dallas* after the series debuted in 1978, rather than a career in feature films. Jane Wyman could have gone down in history as the ex-wife of President Ronald Reagan more than a Hollywood star had it not been for being cast as Angela Channing in *Falcon Crest* in 1981. Stars like Julie Harris, Ruth Roman and Ava Gardner in *Knots Landing*; Barbara Stanwyck in *The Colbys*; and Diahann Carroll in *Dynasty* are a few of the most notable actresses to find new audiences through prime time soap operas.

Lana, in some ways paved the way with one of the first prime time soap operas, *The Survivors*, in 1969. The series failed to draw in the viewers that it needed to survive, and Lana's high-paying salary cost the network dearly when the show failed to deliver. It never finished its first season, ending after a mere 15 episodes due to poor ratings.

Lana thought she was done with television soap operas until she was approached about returning to the small screen after *Falcon Crest* was renewed for a second season in 1981. It would take her to a fictional Northern California winery where drama between battling families hoped to lure in television viewers.

While *Falcon Crest* already had a leading lady in Jane Wyman, it was a far cry from the runaway success of its CBS network sibling show *Dallas*. When *Dynasty* kicked its series into high gear by adding Joan Collins alongside Linda Evans, the show found ratings gold. CBS saw a chance to do the same by casting two warring divas from Hollywood's golden era. The women came from different Hollywood studios with Jane at Warner Bros. and Lana at home at MGM. This time they tackled TV and shared a network.

Crew members recalled a lot of tension in the air when they had scenes to do together, and some gossip reports had claims of spats on the set between the leading ladies. Jane was reported to say that, "Lana has to take a limo to go to the loo," while Lana shot back that

"Jane was almost the 'First Lady.'"  Others say that the tales were just rumors and publicity stunts to get media coverage for the show. Others have suggested that if the quotes were actually uttered at all, they might have just been jokes between the stars at each other's expense. Some say that the two women actually liked and respected one another. Lana reportedly admitted the tales were made up for publicity. "It's a bunch of bull. It's all publicity, trying to drum up a feud between us. I adore Ms. Wyman. I respect her as a lady, an artist and there is no feud."

After Lana's appearance gave a boost to the show, what started as a small guest spot was expanded into a recurring character. By the end of the 1982 season, plans were underway for her to return for the third season.

Lana loved the media attention and fans of the series. During an appearance on *The Phil Donahue Show*, she was thrilled to share with the audience, "Oh, the plans they have for Jacqueline!"

During season three, plans were underway for casting Richard Burton - a man Lana was rumored to have once had an affair with - as her on-screen husband, but the idea was nixed when producers found that the actor's salary demands exceeded what they were willing to pay.

Lana's guest starring role came to an end that season when her character was killed off. The tabloids had a field day suggesting that Wyman had her character axed. Claims that the two women hated each other so much they never spoke off set and that scenes between their characters were filmed separately and spliced together during editing only fueled the rumors.

While it is possible Wyman's control over the production had played a role in the exit of other characters and actors in the series;

Lana and Jane Wyman in a scene from "Falcon Crest."

some suggest if she had any hand in Lana's end, it was possibly because of delays in production and Lana's star behavior on the set. One report suggested that while shooting on location, Turner refused to walk back to her on-site trailer to use "the powder room" during a break in filming, insisting on a limousine on standby at all times, per her contract, including driving her to her dressing room. Some say that Wyman was annoyed when she heard Lana taking credit for the rise in the show's ratings during season two.

Lana put the series behind her and moved on. She knew her career had faded and enjoyed the fact that the show provided some newfound notoriety. She also continued to be open to the possibility that other scripts or projects might come along. When she wasn't in Los Angeles she would travel to Hawaii to see Cheryl or travel abroad. In 1984 she traveled to Egypt and was fascinated by the history and the topic of reincarnation.

When Stephen Crane died in early 1985 of cirrhosis, it was suspected that years of drinking heavily led to his condition. Of his five wives, some say Lana was his one true love. Though the two remained in touch during the years after their divorce – in large part because they shared a child – the two were not in frequent contact during the last years of his life. Cheryl relocated back to the states, settling down in San Francisco, so she could be closer to her father and mother.

Cheryl decided to write a book on her life in the late 1980s. Published in 1988, the book gave Cheryl the chance to detail what it was like to be the daughter of a movie goddess. It also detailed the abuse she suffered at the hands of her stepfather; her relationships with her father and grandmother; accepting herself as gay and her relationship with Josh; and most of all, the events surrounding the death of Johnny Stompanato.

Cheryl's book, *Detour*, was a big success. Cheryl at last faced the past and came out on the other side of history. Lana was able to accept the book, having already had her own chance to tell her side of history. She and Cheryl moved on with Lana occasionally visiting her in San Francisco, or Cheryl heading back to Los Angeles.

Lana also got a chance to work in 1985 when she starred in the two-part series finale of *The Love Boat* during its eigth season. Airing that May, the finale would mark the last major acting appearance of Lana on television.

TWENTY
EIGHT

"I would rather lose a good earring than be caught without make-up."

- Lana Turner

After battles against cancer, Lana earns one last tribute and takes on one final performance - as herself - before the end.

THE END FOR LANA

By the 1990s, Lana had become more of a recluse. Her acting opportunities had dried up, and her health had deteriorated. She wasn't as active as she had been and traveled less frequently. Also, with the lack of a husband or companion, she decided it was best to recede from the Hollywood life. "I don't want people looking at me, saying, 'What's happened to her? God, she's old!' I want my fans to remember me as I was."

After being diagnosed with throat cancer in May 1992, she was finally forced to quit smoking. A long-time smoker, Lana had a hard time staying away from her bad habit - so much so, that there

were times when her cigarettes were actually airbrushed out of photographs of her. She was once even a spokesperson for Lucky Strike
cigarettes.

At first, she refused the recommended chemotherapy treatments, because she feared it was likely to make her hair fall out. She
avoided it for months until
Cheryl convinced her it was
the only way to beat the cancer.
She eventually acquiesced and
began radiation treatments. In
August, columnist Liz Smith
reported that Lana had completed eight weeks of radiation
therapy on a malignant tumor
in her throat.

Down to less than 100
pounds, she told the press she
had finally beaten her addiction to cigarettes and was at
last cancer-free. Despite her
claims, the cancer returned in
July 1994.

Before cancer got the
better of her, Lana made one
last major public appearance
when she agreed to travel to
Spain to accept the Donostia
Lifetime Achievement Award for her long and successful career at the
San Sebastian International Film Festival in September 1994.

In addition to the award, the event was featured in a November 1994 episode of *Lifestyles of the Rich and Famous*. The TV
episode featured Lana talking about her life and career as well as

accepting the award. Turner admitted that she had decided to stop drinking, to eat organic food, and to focus on her spiritual well being for whatever time she had left in her life. She also claimed that she had remained celibate after her final divorce.

By early 1995, the cancer began taking a heavier toll on her health. Her jaw and neck became severely swollen, which was typical for patients with oral and throat cancers. After she began to have

trouble eating, her weight dropped below 92 pounds. Eventually, the cancer became so severe that Lana had to be fed through a stomach tube. Her weight dropped to 85 pounds. She was in great pain. She had no visitors except for her daughter, and was mostly cared for by her maid, Carmen Lopez Cruz.

On June 29, 1995 at the age of 74, Lana Turner died at home in Century City, Los Angeles. Her remains were cremated.

Cheryl inherited much of Lana's personal effects and $50,000 from her estate. Her estate was rumored to be worth some $1.7 million. Aside from Cheryl's bequeathment, the bulk of the money was left to Cruz, who she considered as much a companion as she was a maid for the past 45 years. Lopez was also the primary caregiver during her illness. Cheryl challenged the will, and some reports suggest that most of the estate went to probate costs, legal fees and Lana's medical bills, with little left to fight over.

TWENTY
NINE

"I expected to have one husband and seven babies. Instead, I had seven husbands and one baby."

- Lana Turner

Through the illusion - the smoke and mirrors of Hollywood - the legend of Lana Turner, both in front of and behind the screen, lives on for the ages.

CLOSING REMARKS

"My life has been a series of emergencies," Lana Turner once remarked, reflecting back on her life. And while it's easy to see life through a series of scandals, heartaches, and emergencies, in retrospect, her life was much more than that.

As a child of the 1920s and 30s, her life as a Hollywood starlet began at 16 years old in 1937; and she never really left the spotlight. By the 1950s, many of her contemporaries had worn out their welcome. No longer starlets, many found themselves having to compromise in order to keep working. And as the work grew less lucrative and lighter in quality, careers that once held such promise now seemed desperate and sad. But Lana survived.

As one of the most popular and successful Hollywood stars of the golden era, she also had a prodigious appetite for men. Married eight times to seven different men, she was known for her sexual conquests. While today's celebrity culture makes the 1950s look tame, Hollywood had a reputation as a hotbed of sexuality compared to prim and proper American suburbia. Lana Turner was the woman most women wanted to be, and most men wanted to be with.

Lana Turner, the star, faded from public view in her later years, not wanting her fans to see her as she aged.

Lana was unique. Her career and stardom in many ways were built on publicity. Her personal life, romances, and love affairs were what the average moviegoer thrived on. While many celebrities shied away from the limelight, Lana thrived on it.

Still, 1950s Hollywood was a controlled chaos, with powerful studios like MGM able to squash stories about Lana's abortions, extramarital love affairs, drunken episodes or shoddy behavior. However, as the studio system began to crumble, Hollywood stars found themselves having to fend for themselves in order to keep the public on their side. Tabloids like *Confidential* magazine were built on the public's desire to see the other side of celebrity. Lana herself was unable to hide from *Confidential*, which reported on her often. In fact, Lana could have been the magazine's poster girl. And when everything was all but lost, she somehow managed to turn scandal into gold.

MGM said she was washed up. She showed them they were wrong with an Oscar nomination as Best Actress in one of the top movies of 1957. Behind only *Bridge on the River Kwai, Peyton Place* was the second most successful movie of the year, bringing in more than $16 million at the box office. Though she had weathered that storm, another darker storm rolled in.

On that night of April 4, 1958, standing in her lavish pink bedroom, holding a bloody kitchen knife, with a dead lover lying on her plush pink carpet, she again must have wondered if she could weather this storm.

Protecting her daughter, she mustered up the strength to air her dirty laundry, to admit her mistake in bringing Johnny Stompanato into their lives; and to take the witness stand to recount the horrific events that led to her lover's death. A tragic series of circumstances that led to a grown man – with connections to the Los Angeles mob – to be killed at the hands of her 14-year-old daughter. It seemed almost unreal.

Lana recounted the killing in what some called the greatest performance of her life and career. By the end of the coroner's inquest, the matter was closed with a verdict of justifiable homicide. Lana's public forgave her for what some saw as poor parenting skills, bad decisions and falling for the wrong sort of man.

Instead of drawing inward and dropping out of sight, Lana returned to work and found herself with the most financially rewarding film of her career with *Imitation of Life*. The film would earn her millions and set her up for the rest of her life. With her newfound success, she continued working through the 1960 and 70s. By the 1980s, she reinvented herself as a television star, finding a new audience as one of the stars of *Falcon Crest*. She conquered film, television and stage. And while the work wasn't always critically acclaimed or box office bonanza, her fans never deserted her. They probably never will.

Now - more than 20 years after her death and nearly 60 years since the awful night in 1958 that threatened to ruin her or end her life - the luster and fascination of Lana Turner lives on.

730 North Bedford Drive as it appears today.

THIRTY

It was romance I wanted, kisses and candle-light, that sort of thing. I never did dig sex very much."

- Lana Turner

The career and work of Lana Turner on film

FILMOGRAPHY

1980s

1985 The Love Boat (TV series)

1982-1983 Falcon Crest (TV series)

1980 Witches' Brew

1970s

1976 Bittersweet Love

1975 Persecution

1971 The Last of the Powerseekers (TV movie)

1960s

1969-1970 The Survivors (TV series)

1969 The Big Cube

1966 Madame X

1965 Love Has Many Faces

1962 Who's Got the Action?

1961 Bachelor in Paradise

1961 By Love Possessed

1960 Portrait in Black

1950s

1959 Imitation of Life

1958 Another Time, Another Place

1958 The Lady Takes a Flyer

1957 Peyton Place

1956 Diane

1955 The Rains of Ranchipur

1955 The Sea Chase

1955 The Prodigal

1954 Betrayed

1954 Flame and the Flesh

1953 Latin Lovers

1952 The Bad and the Beautiful

1952 The Merry Widow

1951 Mr. Imperium

1950 A Life of Her Own

1940s

1948 The Three Musketeers

1948 Homecoming

1947 Cass Timberlane

1947 Green Dolphin Street

1946 The Postman Always Rings Twice

1945 Week-End at the Waldorf

1945 Keep Your Powder Dry

1944 Marriage Is a Private Affair

1943 Du Barry Was a Lady (uncredited)

1943 Slightly Dangerous

1943 Strictly G.I. (short)

1942 Somewhere I'll Find You

1941 Johnny Eager

1941 Honky Tonk

1941 Dr. Jekyll and Mr. Hyde

1941 Ziegfeld Girl

1940 We Who Are Young

1940 Two Girls on Broadway

1930s

1939 Dancing Co-Ed

1939 These Glamour Girls

1939 Calling Dr. Kildare

1938 Dramatic School

1938 Rich Man, Poor Girl

1938 Four's a Crowd

Passerby (uncredited)

1938 Love Finds Andy Hardy

1938 The Adventures of Marco Polo

1937 The Great Garrick

1937 Topper (uncredited)

1937 They Won't Forget

Appendix

"A successful man is one who makes more money than a wife can spend. A successful woman is one who can find such a man."

- Lana Turner

SOURCES

Selected Bibliography

A number of books, magazines, newspapers, documentaries and interviews, as well as the films themselves provided sources of information and factual data that went into the writing of this book. Thank you to the many sources referenced throughout the book. There were many individuals whose work, insights, reviews, comments and suggestions that also helped make this book possible.

Books

Anger, Kenneth. *Hollywood Babylon*. Simon and Schuster. 1975.

Bacon, James. *Hollywood is a Four Letter Town*. Avon Books. 1976

Crane, Cheryl. *Detour: A Hollywood Story*. Arbor House. 1988

Crane, Cheryl. *Lana: The Memories, The Myths, The Movies*. Running Press. 2008.

Eames, John Douglas. *The MGM Story*. 1989. Portland House.

Ellen Wayne, Jane. Lana: The Life and Loves of Lana Turner. St. Martin's Press, New York. 1995.

Finler, Joel. *The Hollywood Story*. Crown Publishers. 1988.

Fujiwara, Chris. "The World and Its Double - The Life and Work of Otto Preminger". Faber and Faber Inc., New York. 2008.

Hamilton, George. *Don't Mind if I Do*. Touchstone, Simon & Schuster. 2009.

Hirschhorn, Clive. *The Universal Story*. Crown Publishers. 1983.

LaGuardia, Robert and Arceri, Gene. *Red*. McMillan Publishing. 1985.

McCaffrey, Donald W. " The Road to Comedy: The Films of Bob Hope". Praeger, Westport CT. 2005.

Morella, Joe and Epstein, Edward Z. *Lana: The Public and Private Lives of Miss Turner.* Citadel. 1971.

Munn, Michael. *The Hollywood Murder Casebook.* St. Martin's Press. 1987.
Otash, Fred. *Investigation Hollywood.* Henry Regnery Company. 1976.

Parish, James Robert. *The Hollywood Book of Death.* Contemporary Books, McGraw-Hill. 2001.

Pfeiffer, Lee and Lisa, Philip. The Films of Sean Connery. Citadel Press. 2001.

Root, Eric and Crawford, Dale. *The Private Diary of My Life with Lana.*
Newstar Press. 1996.

Spada, James. *More than a Woman.* Bantam Books. 1993.

Staggs, Sam. "Born to Be Hurt: The Untold Story of Imitation of Life." St. Martin's Press, New York. 1997.

Tosches, Nick. *Dino.* Dell Publishing. 1992.

Turner, Lana. Lana: The Lady, the Legend, the Truth. E. P. Dutton. 1982.

Valentino, Lou. *The Films of Lana Turner.* Citadel Press. 1976.

Magazines, Newspapers and Transcripts

Jones, Jack. "Lana Will Tell Today How Stompanato Died." *The Los Angeles Times,* April 11, 1958.
Scott, Paul. "How Sean Connery Seduced a Movie Legend and Faced the Wrath of the Mafia." *The Daily Mail*, August 11, 2008.

Staff. "Lana Turner: The Fred Otash Files. Hollywood reporter. June 6, 2013.

Staff. Los Angeles Times. "Judy Garland faces arrest on tax evasion." April 3, 1958.

Staff. "Groucho Marx, Richard Diamond, Dragnet and the Real Mc-Coys on TV." *The Los Angeles Times*, April 3, 1958.

Staff. "Judy Garland Gems, Gowns Held After She Fails to Make Bail." *The Los Angeles Times*, April 4, 1958.

Staff. "Local Churches conducted Good Friday Masses from noon to 3 p.m on Friday." *The Los Angeles Times*, April 3, 1958.

Staff. "Bob Hope to Pen book About Trip to Russia." *The Los Angeles Times*, April 4, 1958..

Staff. "Daughter of Lana Turner Kills Man." *The Los Angeles Times*, April 5 1958.

Staff. "Slaying." *The Los Angeles Times*, April 5, 1958.

Staff. "Child Acted Out of Fear, Says Geisler." *The Los Angeles Times*, April 5, 1958.

Staff. "Lana's Daughter Held in Slaying." *The Los Angeles Times,* April 6, 1958.

Staff. "Principals and Associated in Lana Turner Friend's Killing." *The Los Angeles Times* ,April 6, 1958.

Staff. "Stompanato Brother Here to Claim Body of 'Adonis." *The Los Angeles Times,* April 6 1958.

Staff. "Cheryl Turned Over to Police Once Before." *The Los Angeles Times*, April 6, 1958.

Staff. "Stompanato's Brother Wearied by Red Tape." *The Los Angeles Times,* April 7, 1958.

Staff. "On Occasion John said he would cut my face with a razor." *The Los Angeles Times,* April 7, 1958.

Staff. "Lana Turner's 'Love' For Stompanato." *The Los Angeles Times,* April 7, 1958 .

Staff. "Lana Turner's Daughter Ordered Held Until Death Hearing." *The Los Angeles Times,* April 8, 1958.

Staff. "Mickey Cohen found guilty of hitting waiter." *The Los Angeles Times,* April 8, 1958.

Staff. "Stompanato's Book Lists Top Film Names." *The Los Angeles Times,* April 8, 1958.

Staff. "Lana Turner Breaks into Sobs on Leaving Daughter's Hearing." *The Los Angeles Times,* April 8, 1958

Staff. "Cohen Discloses Lana's Love Notes to Johnny" by Jack Jones LA Times April 9, 1958.

Staff. "Angry Mickey Cohen Tells About Lana's Love Letters" LA Times Page 3 April 9, 1958

Staff. "Lana's Fear at Acapulco Told" LA Times April 10, 1958 page 1 by Art Ryon

Staff. "Packs of Letters Vanished Day of Stompanato Death, LA Times page 2 by Jack Jones April 10, 1958

Staff. "Snapshots Hide Lana's Reported Efforts to Break Off Romance? *The Los Angeles Times*, April 10, 1958

Staff. "Strain of Inquest Takes Its Toll." *The Los Angeles Times,* April 11, 1958

Staff. "Cheryl Release Still Undecided." *The Los Angeles Times*, April 12, 1958

Staff. "Lana Unfair, Stompanato Kin Charges." *The Los Angeles Times*, April 11, 1958

Staff. "Coroner's Jury Clears Lana Turner's Daughter." *The Los Angeles Times* April 12, 1958

Staff. "Transcript of the Inquest." *The Los Angeles Times,* April 12, 1958.

Weiler, A.H., "Movie Review: Bachelor in Paradise." *The New York Times*. November 17, 1961

Internet Sources

The Internet Movie Database, www.imdb.com

The Numbers – Box Office Data, Movie Stars, Idle Speculation, www.the-numbers.com

Box Office Mojo, www.boxofficemojo.com

PHOTOGRAPHIC
CREDITS

In addition to the selected bibliography of sources we would also like to acknowledge the many photographs used in this book. While many are part of the author's collection, we would like to specifically acknowledge and thank the following for illustrations used that are used for the purpose of review to highlight and complement the text:

MGM Studios.; 20th Century Fox; Universal; ABC Television; CBS Television; The Los Angeles Times; The Chicago Tribune; The Associated Press.

INDEX

About the Author

John William Law is a writer and journalist whose work has appeared in newspapers, magazines and books. He has worked on the staffs of daily, weekly and monthly publications. He narrates a podcast on iTunes entitled *Behind the Screen with The Movie Files* and has appeared on television and film documentaries discussing film history. He lives in San Francisco. His 2010 book, *Alfred Hitchcock: The Icon Years* was named Best Non-Fiction Biography by Reader's Favorite and his 2014 book *Who Nuked the Duke?* was named Best General Non-Fiction title of 2014 at the San Francisco Book Festival. He was named one of the 50 Great Writers You Should Be Reading in 2015. His books include:

Who Nuked the Duke? (2014, Aplomb Publishing)

What Ever Happened to Mommie Dearest? (2012, Aplomb Publishing)

Alfred Hitchcock: The Icon Years (2010, Aplomb Publishing)

Master of Disaster: Irwin Allen - The Disaster Years (2008, Aplomb Publishing)

Reel Horror - True Horrors Behind Hollywood's Scary Movies (2004, Aplomb Publishing)

Scare Tactics: The Life & Films of William Castle (2002, Writers Club Press)

Curse of the Silver Screen - Tragedy & Disaster Behind the Movies (1999, Aplomb Publishing)

Printed in the USA
CPSIA information can be obtained
at www.ICGtesting.com
LVHW010005220424
778050LV00008B/840